# the Last Salute

### SQN. LDR.
## NUSRAT HUSSAIN (R)

Tellwell Talent
www.tellwell.ca

ISBN
978-1-77370-083-0 (Hardcover)
978-1-77370-082-3 (Paperback)
978-1-77370-084-7 (eBook)

# the Last Salute

*To*

*Abboo Saheb*

*Mr. M.R.Naseem-Abboo Saheb*

On the last day of my service, I went to my father Abboo Saheb, as we called him, and offered him my last salute in the Pakistan Air Force uniform. The seed of the idea to write *The Last Salute* was planted then.

## SQN. LDR. Nusrat Hussain (R)

Abboo Saheb, a well-dressed, handsome, hardworking, strictly disciplined, and honest person started his career as a civilian clerk at the General Headquarters (GHQ) of the Royal British Army in Delhi and Shimla of the un-divided India. He immigrated when Pakistan came into being on August 14, 1947 and continued his service with the GHQ in Rawalpindi, Pakistan. In 1964, when the Capital Development Authority (CDA) was formed to build the new city of Islamabad, he was deputed as Superintendent of the Public Relations Department of CDA which was headed by his longtime friend and famous poet Major Syed Zameer Jaffery. Abboo Saheb rose to Assistant Director serving different departments of the CDA. In 1977, he was deputed further as Director Islamabad Sports Complex's Karachi Division. After retiring from this position, he spent the latter days of life travelling and leading a religious life at his home in Islamabad. He was a well-read and well-travelled person with a fine taste for literature, who occasionally wrote columns for some Urdu newspapers of Pakistan. He performed pilgrimage to Saudi Arabia and visited the United Kingdom, the United States, and Canada.

Abboo Saheb raised his six children from poverty to respectability. He earned his living honestly in an environment where it would have been easy to make money through illicit ways. He will always be the most loving and honourable person who has ever touched my life. After leading a rich and pious life, my father left for his eternal abode on July 4, 2008. He was buried in Islamabad. May the Almighty Allah grant him a higher place in Paradise! Amen.

*Sqn. Ldr. Nusrat Hussain (R)*

# About the Author

Nusrat Hussain is a retired Squadron Leader of the Pakistan Air Force (PAF). He took early release from the Air Force in 1990 after fifteen years of performing the sophisticated jobs of flying, air traffic control, intelligence, and administration. During his tenure with the PAF, he also served a master spy agency: the famous ISI (Inter Services Intelligence) of Pakistan.

Following his release from the PAF, he joined the Bahrain Amiri Air Force (BAAF) in 1992 as an Air Traffic Control Officer. Later, he immigrated to Canada when, in 2001, he established *The Miracle*, the first Muslim newspaper of British Columbia, Canada. Hussain currently lives in Vancouver with his wife Shaheen. They have four children Maheen, Mohammed, Mohib and Mahvish.

# Table of Contents

# Bang–Midair Collision of Mirages!

A Flight Lieutenant at the time, my coursemate Tubrez, survived the midair collision of two mirage aircraft of the Pakistan Air Force (PAF) and lived to tell the tale. He recalls the details of a deadly crash that took place over thirty years ago. Squadron Leader Tahir Afzal, leader of the formation, gave his life in the line of duty.

With over 750 flying hours under his belt, Tubrez was a seasoned fighter pilot. On November 10th, 1983, after having flown a mission in the morning, he was tasked by Group Captain Momin Arif, Officer Commanding (OC) Flying Wing, to prepare a mass brief. The OC was to deliver the brief of the PAF annual exercise 'Jet Stream - 1983'. It is interesting to note, the term OC (Officer Commanding) used by the Pakistan Air Force is similar to the term CO (Commanding Officer) used by the Pakistan army. Tubrez belonged to No. 20 Squadron stationed at Air Base Rafiqui.

His preparation was intercepted by Squadron Leader Tahir Afzal, another squadron pilot who conveyed a message from the OC to hand over the brief to another squadron pilot. Instead, Tahir asked Tubrez to prepare to fly a dissimilar air combat training (DACT) mission against two F-6 aircraft. Tahir, who had recently returned from leave after getting married, looked eager to pair up with Tubrez against the F-6 aircraft.

Squadron Leader Ghazanfar and Squadron Leader Gulrez, the two F-6 pilots, had come from Mianwali Air Base. Before heading back to Mianwali they had requested the DACT mission against the two mirage aircraft. Tubrez considered this a good opportunity to polish his tactics against the F-6s before the start of Phase-3 (actual war condition) of exercise Jet Stream.

A mass briefing was scheduled at 5 pm for the Mirage pilots. The landing time for the ferried F-6s was half an hour before sunset at Mianwali. Both of the interested sets of pilots had a time constraint. They planned that the pair of F-6 aircraft would continue directly to Mianwali after the mission, thereby allowing them to land before sunset. The other set of mirage pilots would land back at Rafiqui and attend the 5 pm briefing.

The mission had originally been planned as 2 versus 2 (2V2) Controller-Versus-Controller (CVC) but was changed to 2 versus 2 (2V2) Visual-Tally at the last minute because of the unavailability of radar.

During a CVC mission the two radar controllers on ground handle the dogfight. One set of aircraft as attackers is managed by one radar controller. The other pair as defenders remains under a different radar controller. Both sets of aircraft operate on separate radio frequencies. The two radar controllers try to position their aircraft at an advantageous position from which point one pilot could visually shoot the other. During training missions, the pilots do not use aircraft fitted with hot guns. When triggered, the cameras fitted with the guns operate by taking cine of the target aircraft. Later on ground, their claims of kill are confirmed by watching the cine.

In a 2V2 Visual-Tally mission, the pilots position themselves by visually observing the other. As such, they have to maintain a good situational awareness.

During the exterior preflight inspection on the ground, Tubrez saw a portion of an electric wire not fully insulated. It was located in the left wheel well under the left fuel tank of his mirage aircraft. He asked the crew chief to have the wire insulated and informed his formation leader on the radio after stepping in the cockpit. The leader, Squadron Leader Tahir Afzal, directed Tubrez to join with the formation in the area after resolving the matter. The two F-6s and the Mirage leader taxied out and took off.

Tubrez had the problem fixed, became airborne, and punched the afterburners to initiate a high rate of climb for a quick join-up with the formation. The formation had already set course for area 'Charlie' (south-west of Atahara Hazari). Tubrez, soon after picking up visual, joined up deep right echelon with his leader.

After entering the area above 25,000 feet, the F-6 formation opened up in battle formation and changed over to their manual frequency. They headed west and waited for the mirages to commence attack.

Tahir and Tubrez climbed above 30,000 feet. Once ready, Tahir committed by calling in and dived on the F-6s fleeing at high speeds. He quickly positioned himself astern the F-6 on the right. Meanwhile, Tubrez observed the fight visually from above in the battle area. As Tahir closed into missile firing range, the two F-6s executed a defensive maneuvre and turned hard right. Their aircraft had the power to turn hard due to their high speeds. This put Tahir at a high angle-off, depriving him from being able to take a valid missile shot. Tahir called-off and exited west from the fight.

With the F-6s bleeding away their energy during the turn, Tubrez tried to get in a position to threaten them further and if possible get a kill shot. He maintained a good height advantage and turned eastwards behind the F-6s. He then dove to their 6 o'clock position and accelerated to almost supersonic speed. He made an effort to swiftly get into a good firing range behind the aircraft on the right, but the F-6 formation picked him up, and in defence, went into a break (maximum 'g' turn) to the right. Tubrez chased, but quickly realizing the increasing angle-off, decided to call-off the attack. He reversed left to exit the fight so that his leader could call in and take advantage of the dying speed state of the target F-6 aircraft.

As he reversed bank, he heard a loud thudding noise on the left side of the aircraft. He thought the left fuel tank had exploded, presuming the wire earlier insulated on the ground had short-circuited. Inside the cockpit, the aircraft controls became stiff. He tossed up and down violently in his seat and his helmet hit against the top and sides of the canopy. Very hot gasses gushed into the cockpit from the left side where he had his hand on the throttle. The aircraft was darting through the sky at near to supersonic speed. His senses were fast losing orientation of the horizon. The aircraft rapidly started falling down from above twenty thousand feet.

The negative g's greyed-out his vision and his hands couldn't go up to pull the main ejection seat handle from above his helmet. Unable to reach the above handle, he went for the alternate ejection pin installed in between his legs at the bottom of his seat. He bent down and pulled it. Blinded under discomforting 'g' forces, and incapable of feeling the ejection jerk, he wasn't sure whether the ejection had worked.

Although he felt the fall with a high rate of descent, he didn't know if he was in or out of the cockpit. He prayed for a miracle as many thoughts went through his mind during that short time. Then he felt a positive tug from over his head. It had worked. He had been thrown out of the cockpit at close to Mach 1 speed and from eighteen thousand feet above the ground. This became a high-speed, high altitude ejection.

He free fell with the seat from 18,000 feet down to 12,000 ft. At 12,000 feet the barometric setting in the seat launched the seat separation followed by the blossoming of the parachute. The parachute converted the free fall into a gradual descent. Now there was comparative silence except for the roaring sound of an aircraft. This was from the F-6s orbiting around him while he descended. The F-6s relayed his exact position to the Rafiqui Air

Traffic Control Tower for the dispatch of the rescue helicopter and departed for their home base in Mianwali. Limited fuel endurance of the F-6s didn't permit them to stay longer over the crash site.

Tubrez shivered with the cold air at that altitude. He wanted to make sure of the proper functioning of the ejection system and deployment of the chute above his head. He glanced up with partial vision and was glad to see the orange roof above him. The chute had deployed perfectly with him still dangling under it. Slowly the chute stabilized, taking him down on its way to Mother Earth.

When he took a look at himself after recovering full vision, the sight of his left hand horrified him. It had burned from the back of the palm up to the forearm. High-speed ejection with no face-blind protection had blown away his helmet. The main ejection handle would have a face-blind pulled in front of his helmet to protect him from the high-speed air blast after ejection. This provision was not available for Tubrez as he had ejected by pulling the alternate ejection handle installed at the bottom. His lip was bruised and cut from the microphone in the mask abruptly pulling away with the helmet. His gloves had blown away with not a thread to be seen. The g-suit had torn from the left side and he had lost his wristwatch as well. Later on the ground, he also noted that his hair was scorched and eyes were bloodshot. High airspeed ejection had taken its toll on him. I remember seeing Tubrez sometime after his ejection in Karachi. We made fun of his hair that had grown grey with the high speed high altitude ejection.

Tubrez could see the Trimmu Headworks (located at the confluence of Jhelum and Chenab rivers) east of him and long stretches of open fields with some scattered village complexes. When he came down further, he saw villagers converging towards him from all directions. A couple of tractor trolleys filled with people could also be seen rushing to the expected drop zone. As he neared the ground, he reminded himself about the parachute landing fall (PLF) he had been taught back at the Academy. Finally hitting the ground with an awkward jerk, he detached the parachute and stood up at once to find himself surrounded by many caring villagers, young and old, who warmly welcomed him.

He asked them to spread his orange chute open for the rescue helicopter to find his position and went into a nearby house. Dust rose because of the stampede. The excitement and rush of so many people were likely to harm his open burn wounds. Someone from a nearby clinic brought two tubes of 'Burnol' and spread the ointment all over his burns.

Tubrez would never forget the kindness and concern of all those who received him on the ground. Some of the people told him about the wreckage of another aircraft lying a few miles away. He could not understand this mention of another aircraft. Tubrez thought they were likely confused by the many disintegrated pieces of his own aircraft. Thirty minutes later he boarded the rescue helicopter and came to know about the crash of the other mirage aircraft. He realized for the first time the disastrous accident was a midair collision with his leader.

The helicopter landed at the base almost at sunset. He was received by the Base Commander Air Commodore Saeed Kamal and many others. The Base Commander comforted and congratulated him as he disembarked on a stretcher. An ambulance took him to the hospital where he remained two weeks undergoing treatment for the burns. This was followed by six months of 'unfitness to fly' by the Central Medical Board (CMB) at the Masroor Air Base. Undoubtedly, by the grace of Allah Almighty, Tubrez had miraculously survived and he returned to the cockpit by April, 1984. He went on to fly another 2,700 hours on various types of aircraft and, after a successful career, retired as an Air vice-marshal in 2010.

A thorough accident investigation later explained the big thudding noise. All things considered, the explosion of the left fuel tank by Tubrez was in fact the collision impact of the other mirage aircraft. According to Tubrez, the investigation concluded that while Tubrez was still in the attack, his leader also entered the fight, probably looking for an opportunity to shoot down an aircraft in visual contact. This was the same aircraft engaged by Tubrez. Their flight paths had converged. Tahir did not pick out his number two and came in from the above rear about seven to eight o'clock, presumably at supersonic speeds. Only supersonic speed could cover this distance.

Large portions of the left wings of both aircraft were found intact after the accident. Tubrez presumed that his leader picked him late when he (Tubrez) was reversing. From above, the leader then rolled sharply left to pull away; he was probably inverted above Mach 1 speed when the left wing of his aircraft struck the left wing of Tubrez's aircraft. We would never know why Squadron Leader Tahir Afzal could not eject. He embraced martyrdom in the line of duty. Squadron Leader Tahir Afzal had gotten married a month before the crash and had lived with his newlywed wife in the shelter accommodation of the Base Officers' Mess. Tubrez, his wife Nageen, and their seven-month-old daughter Ambereen shared a house with Squadron Leader Liaqat Shah and his wife. Incidentally, at the time of the accident, the wives were having their winter afternoon tea out on the lawn of Liaqat Shah's house. Little did they know what was happening up in the air.

Squadron Leader Tahir Afzal was a handsome and friendly officer of the Air Force. I happen to have shared the same bachelor officers' block 9 with him during my first posting at Masroor Air Base in Karachi. I remember many happy meetings with him where we laughed at the top of our voices sharing a joke or an innocent anecdote of our bachelor life.

Tubrez won the ground subject trophy and gold medal on graduation and was a top graduate at the Flying Instructor School (FIS) and F-16 conversion. He led the prestigious Sherdil formation of Risalpur and remained an instructor pilot on Mirage and F-16 aircraft. Thrice, he received the Chief of Air Staff (CAS) commendation certificate and was awarded Sitara-e-Imtiaz, Military SI(M) and Hilal-e-Imtiaz, Military HI(M) before retiring as an Air vice-marshal.

*Tahir Afzal*

*Tubrez Asif*

# *Prologue*

The number of soldiers lost in any war is much higher than the number of officers belonging to the Army and the Navy. However, the trend is reversed when it comes to the Air Force. Fighter pilots die more frequently, not only in war, but also throughout their training and routine flying operations during peace time.

I joined the Pakistan Air Force (PAF) to become a fighter pilot. Unfortunately, my suspension from flying took me away from facing grave dangers in the air. Nevertheless, I remained a fighter pilot at heart and continued extracting exciting adventures right through to my grounded profession as an Air Traffic Controller and an Intelligence Officer.

*The Last Salute* carries stories of my often playful behaviour in the Air Force. At the same time, it describes many adventures of the fighter pilots of the PAF. The crash of *Pakistan One*, carrying General Zia-ul-Haq President of Pakistan, is detailed in the subsequent pages including thrilling stories of ejections out of the cockpits. Several tragic crashes of my comrade friends are also included. Heroes die young. While writing these pages, I have often cried while smiling, remembering my comrades who are no longer in this world.

*The Last Salute* occupied the hard drive of my mind for over 26 years before the words spilled onto the screen of my laptop. On the morning of May 7, 2016, a heart attack took me to the hospital in Langley, British Columbia, Canada, while I was still working on the book. My passion for writing this book ignored many healthy practices. Sleepless nights, unhealthy food, avoidance of exercise, and skipping medicine became contributing factors.

Do not consider my book an autobiography. Autobiographies are inclined to praise the self. On the contrary, on several occasions, I will appear as a mischievous character, though I consider myself playful. In my mind, I was playing with life.

Life is full of shades and cannot be termed as black and white nor as good and bad. In reality, every good person has an element of bad and every bad individual carries a component of good. I have tried to frankly reveal both factors of good and bad.

All the stories contained in *The Last Salute* are original and true as known to me or confirmed by interviewing witnesses. Before writing their stories, I spoke personally to most of the officers first. Then, these stories were returned to them for confirmation as to the accuracy of their information. Some vital information has been held back without disturbing the crux of the matter.

People serving the armed forces of any country may relate these incidents to their own military experiences. Civilians curious to learn more about military life will be amused. This book might emerge as a memoir as it records my service with two different Air Forces, but I prefer to call this collection of memories the impressions and experiences of me, my comrades, and my superiors. This is the way I treat life.

Overall, this is an abstraction of a life lived to the fullest, on the edge, and on my own terms. Like Frank Sinatra sang, this is "My Way":

## The Last Salute

*I've lived a life that's full*
*I travelled each and every highway*
*And more, much more than this*
*I did it my way.*

**Nusrat Hussain**
**Cloverdale, BC.**
**Canada**
**June, 2017**
**nh.guidingstar@gmail.com**

# Chapter One
## Joining the Pakistan Air Force

To become an Air Force fighter pilot was the dream of every young Pakistani man of my generation. I was no exception! After long years of struggle, my dream came true. I was selected to become a fighter pilot in the Pakistan Air Force (PAF). The prayers of my parents and well-wishers were answered.

My late father, whom we called Abboo Saheb, was a follower of the 'Naqshbandi' school of thought in religion. Before appearing for my final selection test he took me to his Pir Saheb, a spiritual man who lived in Haripur, a couple of hours drive from Islamabad. I had met the Pir Saheb only once in my life and remember him as Hazrat Saheb. His graceful white-bearded face glowed with spiritual radiance. He glanced at me only once and continued with his prayers. I did not believe in spirituality then, but my heart seriously registered that single deep and kind glance. He did not speak a single word to me during my stay at his place, but I am now convinced by intuition and several life experiences that my selection by the PAF was because of the acceptance of the prayer of Hazrat Saheb.

Thousands of young men applied for selection. Candidates went through different stages: written exams, interviews, and medicals were conducted in all the different major cities of Pakistan. After clearing the early tests, the successful candidates reported before the Inter Services Selection Board (I.S.S.B.) in Kohat, about seventy kilometres from Peshawar. Candidates stayed there for four days and nights, where their mental and physical abilities were tested. Successful candidates underwent another thorough medical exam at the Central Medical Board, also known as the C.M.B., in Karachi. After gaining the final medical clearance, the General Headquarters in Rawalpindi approved the top names and finally sent out letters to the successful candidates. After going through the detailed selection procedure for the 65th G.D.(P.) [General Duties (Pilot)], Course of the PAF, only twenty-eight boys were selected out of the many thousands of applicants. We reported for initial training at the Lower Topa base of the Air Force on the 13th of October, 1975.

## Air Base Lower Topa

Lower Topa Air Base is located a few miles north of Murree, a famous hill resort in Pakistan. Thousands of tourists from all over Pakistan visit the famous Murree hills during summer to beat the scorching heat of the plains and to enjoy the snow in the winter.

The Air Force established the base in the early nineteen fifties as a public school, but converted it into a temporary training school for officers of the Air Force during the mid-seventies. It never achieved the official status of an academy. The Air Force used it for early training of officers from different ground branches and for pilot ground training.

Trainees from other branches were known as cadets, and trainees to become pilots were called Flight Cadets. I already had some friends who served in the academies of the defence forces. Their anecdotes about academy life had given me an idea about senior-junior relationships. Their stories attracted me like boyhood adventures. The Air Force, however, soon taught me the real difference between fiction and fact.

Wing Commander Altaf Sheikh commanded the Lower Topa Base. He was a bomber pilot - smart, handsome, feared, but largely loved by all the cadets. Next in command was the Officer Commanding (O.C.), Cadet's Wing, named Squadron Leader Frank D'Silva. He reported to the Base Commander on discipline, ground training, and other activities of the officers, cadets, and Flight Cadets at the base. Under his command were two brilliant officers: Flight Lieutenant Faheem Baig, the Squadron Commander of No.1 Squadron; and Flight Lieutenant Mujeeb commanded the cadets of No. 2 Squadron. Flying Officer Gulaster Minhas was the officer in charge of General Service Training (GST). He was a hardworking and physically fit officer admired and loved by the cadets. Under his command were the drill staff consisting of non-commissioned instructors who conducted our drill and basic pistol and rifle firing.

# Landing of the Eagle

On the first reporting day at Lower Topa, I was dropped off by my two friends, then Captain Shahid Hussain and ex-flight cadet Mohsin Raza; as well as by my brother, Ishrat Hussain. Usual treatment for new cadets did not begin for me while they remained there, but as soon as they left, many senior Flight Cadets rushed at me shouting from all directions. Not understanding anything, confused and in a panic, I stood there like a deer caught in the headlights. They asked me my name. A simple response of "Nusrat Hussain" was not acceptable to them. I had no clue what they wanted to hear. After calling me many insulting names, they told me to always insert the title Flight Cadet before my name. The pride of this instant title brought great joy to my heart and lifted my energy. I took their harsh treatment with dignity and without showing any hurt.

Becoming a part of the Pakistan Air Force induced an instant honour. I learned that a flight cadet was a future pilot belonging to the elite General Duties Pilot G.D.(P.) branch of the Air Force. Senior Flight Cadet Tanvir Mohajir from 63rd G.D.(P.) course, who proclaimed to be the biggest terror on the base, took me under his wing. He asked me to frog-jump the stairs to the first floor of the building opposite the cadets' mess. There were about fifteen concrete steps. When I reached the top, he ordered me to start front-rolling down from the top of the stairs. My back hit the concrete edge of the steps after completing every roll. I felt hurt, yet the honour of Flight Cadet attached to my name forbade me from showing any signs of pain. That night Senior Mohajir took me on a tour of the cadets' mess. I kept front-rolling as he announced the different buildings coming at us right and left.

It wouldn't be fair not to mention the treatment awarded to Senior Mohajir on the Golden Night. Golden Night is the night before graduation, when the seniors are traditionally declared juniors for a couple of hours. I told my coursemates not to touch Mohajir; he was all mine. I made him front roll on broken glass pieces spread out like a bed sheet on the floor. He boldly obeyed my commands. I was so impressed that I picked him up on my shoulders and took him around the mess at the end of the Golden Night.

I compared the lost freedom of the civilian life I had left behind to the instant honour of a Flight Cadet. Freedom and honour carried a special place in my heart and I was not prepared to part with either. I decided to extract maximum advantage from both.

# Drum Out

One of the new Flight Cadets was drummed out in our first week of reporting to the base. He could not cope with the physical and mental pressures of training and deserted the base. That was considered a big crime. He was arrested, brought back to the base by the Air Force Police, and drummed out of the academy. Drumming out is a humiliating experience. All the cadets formed two parallel lines stretching from the cadets' mess to the outside guardroom gate. Down the walkway between the files, a drummer beating a drum walked behind the culprit, who marched in front of the lined up cadets carrying his baggage placed above his head.

The disgraced cadet then had to pass through the walkway with the sound of drums and the claps of the lined up cadets. They removed his ranks before sending him out of the main gate of the guard room. This ceremony also served as a warning for the remaining cadets.

# Casino Night

During junior cadetship, we performed guard duty with a G3 rifle by patrolling around the cadets' mess at night. The G3 rifle carried a distinguished name in the weapons' industry. It was magazine-fed and used a delayed blowback action designed by German engineers. It weighed about four kilograms and could fire single shots or bursts of fire like a machine gun. One night when on guard duty outside the seniors' barracks, I noticed a dim light coming out of one of the windows. When I peeked in the window, I saw some seniors playing cards by candlelight. The money placed between them confirmed that they were gambling. Some seniors of the gambling ring liked my naughty attitude and my brave facing of the punishments. My reputation with them helped me in becoming a part of this gambling ring. They were playing three-card poker, popularly known as 'Flaash' in Pakistan.

There wasn't much money at stake - everyone played with a maximum of ten rupees. The code name given to this was 'Casino Night'. I considered it an adventure, providing me an opportunity to mix with seniors who were taking a risk by disobeying the rules. I enjoyed risks in life.

Some 'Casino Night' cadets were caught playing by the officer-in-charge of discipline. He summoned the assembly of the entire wing in front of the cadets' dining hall. Flight Lieutenant Faheem Baig conducted an investigation by calling the suspects inside the room individually. Within an hour, he busted the 'Casino Night' gang and identified all the ten culprits. Nine others belonged to the senior courses. I was the only junior flight cadet, with less than a month of service. It made me famous - or infamous, depending on your point of view.

We feared termination from the Air Force, but Air Headquarters took a mild view considering the large number of involved cadets. They awarded us the most severe punishment of getting our heads shaved and putting us all on regular restriction.

Restriction carried the punishments of staying in uniform the whole day and night and no booking out of the base. After packing up from the education directorate, we signed a register at the cadets' guardroom every hour. We were given extra drills twice a day with thirty pounds of haversack on the back and a G3 rifle on the shoulder.

Senior Flight Cadet Rauf, who also had his head shaved, told the juniors about the Phantom Squadron comprised of the 'shaved heads'. He ordered the juniors to give a body shiver whenever they saw a shaved head cadet in the cadets' mess. His announcement restored some pride and, despite the guilt, we enjoyed the punishment of becoming a part of the Phantom Squadron. The company of the Eagles who all possessed great hearts kept me soaring through difficult times. They knew the art of extracting fun even under adverse conditions. The irony of aging is that I now have a bald head. Oftentimes when combing my hair in front of the mirror, I am reminded of the 'Casino Night' adventure.

## The Life of a Junior Cadet

A typical day at Lower Topa started in P.T. kit with early morning assembly known as 'morning jerks', a few-mile run. On return, we changed into our uniforms for breakfast in the dining hall. After breakfast, we marched to the parade ground for drill training with the G3 rifle. From the parade ground, we went to the education directorate for studying different subjects. After packing up from the education directorate, it was time for lunch. After lunch, we attended punishment assemblies that were called by the seniors until the games period in the evening. At the end of games, an individual study period was observed in the barracks. Seniors ensured compliance by visiting the barracks.

After the study period, we reported for dinner in the dining hall. 'After Dinner Literary Activities' (ADLA) conducted in the ante room by the officers provided some time of relief. Stories and poems of famous writers and poets were read out during that time. After ADLA, the punishment assemblies were called again by the seniors. These lasted until late at night. If anyone of us committed a mistake, then the whole course was called for punishment. The collective method of punishment implanted comradeship among the coursemates. Soon we were used to this routine of military life.

We were swiftly promoted to the second - the final term at Lower Topa. Life became relaxed as we became seniors. New intakes arrived, but now our juniors became our victims. This was the amazing roller coaster ride of the military life!

# Dogfight over the Washroom

During the winter break in December 1975, ten Flight Cadets were detailed to attend a ski and snow survival course for two weeks. Air Base Naltar, located about forty kilometres from Gilgit, is a thirty-minute flight from Chaklala. We boarded an Air Force C-130 flight for Gilgit - my first life experience of boarding an aircraft. I had heard about the pretty air hostesses who served delicious food as well as the comfortable, relaxing seats. However, the seating arrangements inside the C-130 aircraft shattered my imagination of a luxurious commercial flight. Inside, the rugged C-130 presented a scene from the prison of a war camp.

We sat tightly tucked in the red-coloured canvas seats that hung from metallic silver bars. Stout technicians of the air force danced freely in the belly of the aircraft while attending to different instruments installed within the airframe. Our ears were deafened with the start-up of the four noisy turboprop engines. Hot air gushed down from above as the aircraft started taxiing out from Air Base Chaklala. General Zia-ul-Haq, President of Pakistan, would eventually die in a C-130 crash. Unbeknown to me at that time, thirteen years later, in 1988, I would be the Duty Air Traffic Controller at Chaklala signing the flight plan of Pakistan ONE carrying the deceased president.

Flying Officer Shabbir Shah, our officer-in-charge, took us to the cockpit of the aircraft. I enjoyed watching the gorgeous scenic view of the snow-covered mountains. The Karakorum hill range stood high on either side of our flight path. Flying over fifteen thousand feet above, one could see the beautiful green and snow-covered valleys below.

After landing at Gilgit Airport, we rushed to waiting jeeps driven by expert local drivers. After half an hour of crazy driving through winding tracks we arrived at the Naltar Air Base. Sitting in the front seat with the driver, I would occasionally view the valleys located hundreds of feet below. It was a thrilling and scary ride, more chilling than the rugged flight of the C-130. Finally, we reached the beautiful snow-covered officers' mess of Naltar.

Group Captain Shah Khan commanded the Air Base Naltar at the time. He was an excellent skier who moved beautifully on his skies. His dedicated loyal batman from Hunza served us with tea on skis while we were up on the slope. A chairlift installed at the ski slopes carried the skiers to the top from where we started skiing.

The officers' mess of Naltar reminded me of scenes from the famous James Bond movies filmed in some parts of Europe. Excellent accommodation carried bedrooms with two beds and an en suite bathroom. Bathrooms were fitted with an electric water geyser which provided hot comfy showers. Flight Cadet Kazim was my roommate during the course at Naltar. He carried a soft and disciplined reputation compared to my carefree, naughty, and ill-disciplined repute. But we jelled in friendship despite the stark differences in our personalities.

The small sized electric hot water geysers in the bathrooms needed some time to heat the water after one person had taken a shower. The general rule of 'first come-first served' applied. The roommate first entering the washroom showered first. Then the second roommate waited for the water to heat up again. Being young and naughty, we often struggled to take the first turn. One day after return from the slopes, I noted that Kazim had already locked the bathroom door. This signaled his firm position without any room for dispute. But then Kazim suddenly unlocked the door and came out to pick up his vest. As he passed by me in the room, I rushed into the bathroom to shower first. He reacted fast and reached the bathroom door before I could lock it. We began to physically struggle and argue. Hearing the noise, a few other coursemates from the adjoining rooms came inside to watch this ensuing hilarious struggle. We stood there fully dressed, each claiming our right to shower first - me inside the bathroom and Kazim with his foot in the door. Kazim claimed that he had entered the bathroom first, but witnesses saw me in and him out of the bathroom. Ground position favoured my claim, but Kazim was right indeed. Before the attending jury passed a verdict, an interesting idea came to my mind and I removed my shirt. Knowing my buddy to be sweet and soft, I was confident that he would run out if I also removed my trousers. I forewarned Kazim of my intent if he didn't leave the bathroom. The jury of my other coursemates encouraged Kazim to hold position and to not give in to my dirty tactics. I counted one, two, and three - Kazim ran out as soon as I dropped my pants. I locked the bathroom door behind the heavy laughter of my lively coursemates. Kazim became a C-130 pilot and retired as an Air Commodore after commanding the Chaklala Air Force Base. He now captains the majestic Airbus for Air Blue airlines in Pakistan.

After completion of the ski course, we spent a night in the beautiful Hunza valley for a snow survival exercise. Squadron Leader Naunehal and Flight Lieutenant Chohan, our ski and snow survival instructors, taught us about survival techniques if ejected in snow-covered surroundings. Equipped with a parachute and a survival kit carrying some rations and a few other important tools of survival, we spent a day and a night in the snow-covered jungle. Watching nature in freezing temperatures under the open sky was truly an excellent experience.

We barely used the shelters that we had made during the day with the help of tree branches which were wrapped in parachutes to save us from the cold air. Instead, we gathered around a big campfire that kept burning the entire night. Wood collected during the day helped to keep us warm. In the morning we walked down a few miles to where waiting jeeps picked us up and brought us back to the comfortable compound of the Naltar mess.

# Boxing Competitions

Inter-squadron boxing competition preparation started a month before the fights. Chief Tech Yaqub was our boxing coach. He prepared me to fight two matches with only an hour's rest between the two fights. I knocked down my first opponent, Flight Cadet Raja Aslam, within the first round. Raja later retired from the service as an Air Commodore.

The second bout was an exhibition match with Flight Cadet Rafaqat Ali that lasted for all three tiring rounds. Ali was a good boxer; moreover, he was a friend. He held the highest Cadet's appointment of Wing Under Officer. Our coach arranged the fight because he thought us to be the most aggressive and stylish boxers of the academy. This bout displayed the most interesting and hard-fought match of the competition. I punched solid on target that made him bleed through his nose. His punches were brutal too, but I managed to keep my face clean.

We fought with aggression. Forty years later, in my honest opinion, the fight should have been a draw pronouncing both winners. However, the judges declared me a winner on points. But that night, despite losing the fight, Ali won many hearts including mine. After being declared a winner, I hugged him tight. As I slowly walked back towards my corner, Ali came running from behind and picked me up on his shoulders by passing his head through my walking legs. He took a round of the whole ring by keeping me on his shoulders. He displayed a great spirit of sporting behaviour and comradeship.

I fought five bouts during my cadetship. My opponents were knocked out on three occasions; on the fourth I won on points, and I lost the last fight on points during the Inter-Base Boxing Competition at Air Base Korangi Creek in Karachi. My boxing career ended after graduation as the officers of the Pakistan Air Force are not permitted to participate in boxing.

Ali left the Air Force immediately after graduating as a fighter pilot. Our friendship has lasted with love and respect for over 40 years. Ali lives in New York - I presented him with a framed photograph of our bout when I last visited him a few years ago.

*Nusrat after bout with Raja Aslam*

*Nusrat after bout with Ali*

*65th G.D.(P) Course at Lower Topa*

*After boxing competitions from left standing: Zulfi, Robson,
Amjad, Sohail, Flt. Lt. Gulastar, Sqn. Ldr. Frank D'Silva, Ali,
Flt.Lt. Rizvi, Chf.Tec. Yaqub, Qzi, Nusrat and Zafar Yasin.
Sitting from Left: Adnan, Rizvi, Gardezi,
Hakam, Saqib, Waheed and Kazim.*

*65th G.D.(P) Course with Waqar from 63rd G.D.(P)*

*From Left: Rauf, Gondal and Nusrat*

*Nusrat and Afzaal*

*Nusrat with Mohsin Raza when he was a Flt. Cadet at Lower Topa*

*65th G.D. x-country run. Late Gardezi and Sikander Shah in front. Late Tahir standing behind with other course mates.*

*Nusrat and Pervez at Lower Topa Tea Bar.*

# Chapter Two
## Risalpur Academy

After graduating from Lower Topa, we reported at the Air Force Academy Risalpur for the third term. After enjoying the final term seniority at Air Base Lower Topa, becoming a junior again at Risalpur was an interesting experience. However, it proved different from the junior experience of Lower Topa as, unlike then, everyone was now well aware of the military norms.

PAF Academy Risalpur, about 15 kilometres from Nowshera and across the bank of the Kabul River, is an hour's drive from Peshawar and two-hour's drive from Islamabad. In those days it was the exclusive pilot training academy of the Air Force. Trainee pilots joined Risalpur in the third term and graduated after completing the third, fourth, and final terms.

Air Commodore Datta commanded the academy and Group Captain Imtiaz Bhatti, a pilot of the star fighter F-104 supersonic aircraft, was the OC Cadet's Wing. Wing Commander Shajar was the OC Education Directorate where the ground instructors taught the subjects of aero-engine, thermodynamics, meteorology, navigation, airmanship, and Air Force law. Squadron Leader Bardar Khan commanded the General Service Training (GST) department, responsible for parade, rifle training, and other sporting activities.

# Maulana of the Tea Bar

The small tea bar of the cadets' mess at Risalpur was a favourite evening hangout of the senior Flight Cadets. It could house 15 to 20 people and was usually filled with the smoke of cigarettes and the laughter of the senior flight cadets. Final term cadets enjoyed the privilege of sitting in the tea bar. Juniors entered and exited after a quick purchase of needed items.

Maulana, a tall, grey-bearded, graceful Pathan character kept the tea bar clean. He single-handedly ran the administration and operation of the bar. Though employed as a grade four lascar, he enjoyed great respect from all the senior cadets and the visiting officers. Many senior officers who rose to the ranks of high star generals had passed as ordinary junior flight cadets at Risalpur Academy in front of Maulana. At times, he even checked and warned the junior cadets in response to any inappropriate behaviour. We took it in high spirits.

Maulana often made two coffees: one for me and the other for himself. I paid for his coffee. We smoked as he sat across the bar telling me interesting stories about the cadetships of different senior officers. Maulana spoke in flawless English with a clear accent. Giving respect to those who deserved it was one of the higher morals instilled in us by the Air Force.

# Eagles are Airborne

Flying is unnatural to humans; they are designed to conduct their affairs on the ground. The ambitious nature of man lifted him to fly under the high sky. The Air Force planned flying in a professional progression, starting from a small single engine propeller-driven aircraft to the highest performance multiengine jet planes. In the education directorate, Flight Cadets studied the mechanics of different aircraft in the aero engine class. Thermodynamics taught the effect of different physical forces like lift and drag that acted on the engine and airframe when in the air. Navigation classes taught the calculations involved in preparing maps of the flight routes. Meteorology distinguished between the different weathers affecting flying. Clouds, thunder, lightning, and turbulence were the major areas of interest.

There were two flying squadrons for Flight Cadets at Risalpur. The Primary Flying Training (P.F.T.) was commanded by Squadron Leader Hameed Malik, while Wing Commander Naeem Atta Commanded the Basic Flying Training squadron (B.F.T.). Every qualifying Flight Cadet progressed from the P.F.T. to the B.F.T.

# Flying the MFI-17 Mushshak

P.F.T. squadron consisted of the MFI-17 Mushshak piston aircraft, a dual control fixed-gear basic trainer aircraft manufactured in Sweden. Propelled by a single four-cylinder piston engine, this aircraft had full aerobatic capabilities. In addition to training, it was also used for towing, reconnaissance, and transportation purposes.

Flight Lieutenant Raashid Kalim was my first flying instructor. He later rose to the rank of Air Marshal and served as the vice Chief of Air Staff before retiring from the service. He was a smart man with a soft voice and good manners. He taught me all the flying maneuvres on the MFI-17 Mushshak aircraft. Under his supervision, I learned the basic maneuvres and got my first solo. He taught me the steep turn, aileron roll, barrel roll, roll off the top, and spin and recovery. At times, I vomited during flying and landed with a vomit bag in my hand. It was because of the continuous encouragement of Sir Kaleem that I cleared the Final Handling Test (F.H.T.) and was promoted to fly the T-37 jet aircraft in the B.F.T. squadron.

# Saved from the Edge

In the fourth term booking out was stopped for everyone because the French Air Cadets were visiting the academy. I had promised to meet with some friends in Lahore. In order to honour my commitment, I decided to bunk and absconded. My dear roommate Flight Cadet Amjad Bashir was to cover during my absence. We usually covered for each other during our extracurricular activities. Amjad later graduated as a fighter pilot and retired from the service after rising to the rank of an Air Commodore.

This time, one senior Flight Cadet grew suspicious of my absence. He then visited our room a few times to confirm my absence. Amjad ran out of excuses so I was confirmed out of academy. An investigation revealed that I was absent without official leave from the Academy (AWOL). This would result in termination from the Air Force.

On return, I came to know the bitter truth and feared termination. It was only a few months before graduation. I kept thinking about it all night and in the morning I went to see my Squadron Commander, Flight Lieutenant Hamid (nicknamed Insaan Bhai). He had launched the termination case. I talked to him with tears in my eyes. By dramatizing my false story as a lover boy, I lied. I told him about how the girl I loved was compelled to marry somewhere else by her parents. She had threatened to commit suicide. I took off without leave to tell her parents to wait for my graduation - "I will marry her after becoming an officer." It was the perfect love story narration of a brave soldier of our era.

My tearful acting touched the heart of Flight Lieutenant Hamid. I saw regret in his eyes. At that point, I innocently complained by adding, "Sir, I wish, as a concerned Squadron Commander, you had listened to my reason for absence before initiating the termination case." My ploy was as effective as spraying fuel over his fire of guilt.

He immediately responded, "I am sorry to hear it, young man; let me see how I can undo my action. I have sent your termination case to the Officer Commanding Cadets' wing, but I will go again to him and do my best." I came back happy that my acting had lit a ray of hope.

But Flight Lieutenant Hamid came to my room that evening with a heavy heart and sorrow in his eyes. The OC wing had refused to withdraw the termination case. Hamid advised me to pull some strings if I had them. Since I had none, I silently waited for the final orders.

Another evening of grief had landed when my coursemate, Flight Cadet Malik Hakim, came to my room. He asked me not to worry about anything and said, "They cannot expel you. I promise to quit the Air Force if they terminate you out of the academy." I thought Hakim was emotional and consoling my grief, but he meant every word he spoke that night.

Hakim went to our navigation instructor, Wing Commander Nazar, who was related to him. Nazar was the coursemate of OC Cadets' Wings, Group Captain Imtiaz Bhatti - the only person who could save my termination. Hakim implored Nazar to go to the OC Cadets' wing for reconsideration of my dismissal. Nazar promised to help.

The next day I sat in my class in the education directorate - waiting for my termination orders. To my surprise, Wing Commander Nazar called me out from the class and smiled at me. He told me that he had spoken to the OC Cadets' Wing Group Captain Bhatti, who had agreed to spare me from dismissal and instead punish me with regular restrictions.

I was overjoyed and thanked him. Hakim graduated as a pilot of the C-130 aircraft. He retired as a Group Captain from the service. I owe a lot to the kind gestures of many great friends like Hakim.

After some time, Group Captain Bhatti, OC Cadets' Wing called me to his office. He said, "I have withdrawn your termination because a few people came and talked to me." He nevertheless added, "You will be on Regular Restrictions."

I saluted before leaving his office. I would be on restriction - once again - for the rest of my cadetship at Risalpur.

# Senior Bashir Crashed

Senior Flight Cadet Bashir of 62nd G.D.(P.) was an excellent person with a mellow voice. I always found him to be a kind, smiling senior. One afternoon he took off in a T-37 aircraft for a solo outside the circuit mission. His area of operation was ten thousand feet above Lawrencepur, in the training area. His roommate, senior Flight Cadet Majeed Maleeh, was also on the same mission over Campbellpur in the adjoining practice area. The two eagles probably decided to engage in a low-level formation. Not trained for the mission, senior Bashir lost control of his aircraft and hit the ground close to the big antenna at Lawrencepur. Eye witnesses on the ground reported two planes flying together at low-level. The Air Force authorities interviewed senior Majeed Maleeh and terminated him from the academy.

This event was shocking for all of us. We were young and full of life, with dreams for our future. We were engaged in an activity that carried grave dangers even during times of peaceful training. Apart from the brave nature of the individuals, the driving force behind this dangerous career was our love for our country - to defend the homeland during war.

Senior Bashir's crash that evening created a gloomy atmosphere in the academy. We grieved in our remembrance for someone who had interacted with us regularly. I have lost many young, close friends in air crashes in the Air Force, which I write about in later pages.

# The Aircraft was Heavy!

Academy days were a golden time of dreams and ambitions. We enjoyed the endless ragging, guard duties, and continuous bullshitting by our seniors. Some of us ended in BFT hoping to fly the noisy jet T-37 aircraft. Most of the early days of BFT saw us aspiring pilots running like crazy around the squadron wearing flying coveralls and thick heavy flying shoes. The dream of becoming a fighter pilot was turning into a mirage. A normal day started with tortuous emergency sessions and ended with angry dialogues with our instructors. Finally our flying started and there was respite from the running and ragging.

Flight Lieutenant Arif, who later rose to the rank of Air Marshall, was the Flight Commander of No 2. Squadron. His amazing character, hefty personality, and unlimited energy were often evident around the squadron and the flight lines. It was not uncommon to see the broad, heavily built man lumbering onto the tarmac and chasing the aircraft technicians. His main concern was to have a maximum number of T-37s serviceable. Risalpur's hot summer days or cold frosty winter mornings never deterred him from being on the tarmac ensuring the availability of maximum aircraft.

Flight Lieutenant Arif had a habit of conducting debriefings of missions in the main briefing room. He also ensured that all cadets lounging or sleeping in the changing room attended his debrief sessions. He mistakenly thought that his long debriefs would enlighten the cadets and be helpful in their flying missions. One day he took Flight Cadet Azam, our coursemate, for his solo check clearance. On that day, some of the not flying students were forced into the briefing room. We had to listen to Azam's debriefing session conducted by Flight Lieutenant Arif. Unfortunately for Azam, the mission had not gone well. As Flight Lieutenant Arif fumed, the briefing room sounded with a mixture of flowery Urdu and English jargon. It was a sight to watch the broad-chested instructor bellowing at full voice while the skinny, dejected Azam stood miserably, trying in vain to create an impression that he was understanding the debrief. Finally, towards the end, the instructor repeatedly asked Azam: "Why were you getting low on the final approach?"

One must understand that a student has no logical explanation for 'why.' Azam, terror-stricken, desperately searched for an answer but he could not find a suitable reply. Arif was determined and clearly didn't want to excuse Azam without justifying his poor performance.

Finally, mustering all his courage, Azam blurted out, "Sir, the aircraft was heavy today." There was a deathly silence in the room. His response pointed to the fat body of Arif. It shocked us and left Flight Lieutenant Arif speechless. He looked incredulously at Azam and we could feel that, had he not been in uniform, he would have strangled Azam. Azam's explanation ended the debriefing session and we hurriedly followed our order of getting in the orbit - running around the block with our hands above our heads.

Later we asked Azam why he had replied in that manner. His innocent answer was that with Flight Lieutenant Arif in the seat the aircraft had to be heavy. But, the good part for us was that for the next few days we were spared the debriefing sessions of Flight Lieutenant Arif.

This anecdote of our cadetship flying days was remembered by Yawar. He retired after becoming a fighter pilot and reaching the rank of Squadron Leader. Yawar is a star captain flying the Airbus aircraft. Azam also graduated as a fighter pilot and left the service after becoming a Wing Commander. He practices law in Rawalpindi. Arif retired after rising to the rank of Air Marshal.

# LOST and Found

There is an interesting lost and found anecdote experienced by my coursemate, then Flight Cadet Shahid Mahmud, popularly known as 'Chira' (a male sparrow) because of his love for flying. He was scheduled to fly a solo night navigation mission on the T-37 aircraft. When he came out of the squadron on his way to the flight lines towards the aircraft, he saw Flight Cadet Ejaz Minhas, popularly known as the 'Black Sheep' of the course, running around the block - his instructor scolding him from behind. Minhas had flown the earlier mission, which took off at dusk, and had gotten lost. Radar had guided him back. Now his instructor was making sure he would never again lose sight of Risalpur by having him run around the Squadron building.

Thinking himself a hot rod pilot, Shahid, in his mind added to the joy by comparing the thump of Black Sheep's boots to the sound of a goat on double march. Minhas was called 'Black Sheep' because, on a few occasions of our junior days, he had reported late to the assemblies called by the seniors. His tardiness had resulted in extra punishment for the entire course. These popular names, also termed 'service names', were liberally used to signify lasting love and temporary insult for each other. Everyone took it in high spirits. Frankly speaking, I had earned the service name of 'Nakka' for my big nose.

How could one get lost with all the available navigational aids and by staying in visual contact of that familiar area? Shahid, after the briefing, had further studied the map and noted all the rivers, canals, and tributaries which might shimmer on that moonlit night to steer the course in the intended direction. He took a mental note of all the towns whose flickering lights would assure him to the correctness of route. Brimming with confidence, he shrugged off all apprehensions and headed to the tarmac. "The flight path is familiar. So what if it is nighttime, it's a piece of cake!" he thought to himself as he climbed into the cockpit after carrying out the preflight checks around the aircraft.

A lecture once given by the flight surgeon about psychology of disorientation came to his mind. "You will not trust your instruments even if the compass needle is pointing home." Yet this warning was hard to believe. If you were lost, why would you not trust your instruments? He later realized that in his case, the flight surgeon was spot on.

After getting airborne, he climbed out to Mardan and noticed the lights below dimming fast due to hanging dust in the air. After climbing to the assigned altitude, he set a southeast course for the first leg. He nailed the two navigation points in about fifty minutes and made it back to Mardan. "It was after all, a piece of cake," he congratulated himself. After the descent, he leveled off at two thousand feet and reported his position to the tower. Next up was to look for Risalpur and head home.

"But where is Risalpur? Surely it is only nine miles away from him, but where in the world is it tonight?" He could not spot the Risalpur beacon. He had the rude realization that the fat lady had not sung and his mission was not over after arriving over Mardan.

Risalpur's beacon flashed the Morse code signature "RS" - who could forget dit-da-dit, dit-dit-dit. But that night he did not see the beacon. He was sure he was over Mardan. And he had some sense which way was north, because he could see the vertical outlines of Malakand hills. He estimated a direction and headed in. The darn place was just nine miles south, but he could not see it. He turned back to soon find himself over Mardan again.

"Naiza 857, report position," he heard the Risalpur Control Tower calling him.

"Descending overhead Mardan," he lied. The Control Tower did not question that he had already reported Mardan a while back. "There is no way in the world I am going to be embarrassed and let Black Sheep's punishment befall on me," he reminded himself. On top of that, he would be the laughingstock of the course, if not the academy, if he was unable to get back to Risalpur - just nine miles out.

He had already tuned his instruments to Risalpur and they were pointing in the direction he had just been. "I must have tuned them wrong," he thought, because he had just flown in that direction.

Now, he found himself in somewhat of a panic. As he headed east he soon noticed the gleaming Tarbela Dam. "How stupid I am to come in this direction," he frowned at himself. Soon he was again over Mardan and still could not make out where Risalpur was.

"Naiza 857, report position," called the Control Tower.

He repeated, "Descending over Mardan." Whoever was on duty that night must not have noticed that he had been "descending" over Mardan for a while and still hadn't "hit the ground."

Next he turned north, and as expected, soon came upon the hilltops of Malakand. He turned around and was back over Mardan. He called an emergency meeting of all his intellectual faculties. There was no danger to his life nor to the aircraft he was flying. There was still plenty of fuel. But there was the other matter of honour and blemishing of his unblemished performance during all his navigation missions. The added incentive was his vision of Black Sheep's languid running around the block, a fate that he had to avoid.

Since, in his mind, the aircraft instruments were pointing in the wrong direction, and he had visited Tarbela twice, Malakand once, perhaps Nowshehra as well, where the hell was he in reference to Risalpur? He was sure how his coursemates would respond to his love for staying overhead Mardan.

The reason he could not see Risalpur was because of its invisible beacon. He should have spotted it at ten thousand feet, but at two thousand feet it somehow wasn't visible. Then it hit him. What about the Peshawar beacon? It transmits PS.

He fixed his position with the distant Malakand hills and Mardan, knowing that he was flying east to west. "Peshawar must be at my 11 o'clock." He looked hard and found the faint Peshawar beacon. Now that he had three points, he knew where Risalpur should be and looked that way. He didn't know if the dust over Rislapur had lifted, or settled, but after a long hard stare, he spotted the Risalpur beacon. Just then, this time in a rather stern tone, the tower demanded to be informed of his position. "Heading base," he replied with confidence. Soon he was on the ground.

When he arrived back at the Squadron, Black Sheep had been dismissed. Those who had flown the same mission simply headed back to the transport. Not a soul knew what had transpired with him over Mardan.

Shahid left the Air Force as a Pilot Officer after flying the C1-30 aircraft. He lives in Maryland with his family. Minhas went on to become a successful flight navigator, and was deputed to Saudi Arabia as an instructor. He ended his career as a Group Captain. Minhas lives in Sargodha and is now actively involved in the politics of Pakistan - quite a distance from his languid running around the block that night!

# T-37 Aircraft - Recovery of the Idiot!

Flying Officer Sibghatullah Ahmed Mudassir was my instructor pilot on the T-37 jet trainer aircraft. He was a great professional and a thorough gentleman who treated his students with love and respect. After commanding No.15 Squadron of the PAF, he took early retirement at the rank of Wing Commander. He later piloted the 737 Airbus and Jumbo-747 aircraft for commercial airlines.

The T-37 aircraft, fitted with dual controls, twin jet engines, and retractable gears with full aerobatic capabilities, was considered a comfortable flying car. The pilot carried more paraphernalia on the body than my earlier Mushshak piston aircraft. The helmet overhead had a visor in front of the eyes, contained a headset in the ears, and an oxygen mask covered the nose and the mouth. Fitted inside the mask over the mouth was a radio transmitter. We also carried a parachute on our backs in case of ejection.

To avoid any struggle or confusion over the flight controls between the two pilots, only one person was supposed to fly at any given time. Before taking over the flight controls, the instructor pilot said, "I have the controls."

The student pilot on hearing command took his feet away from the rudders, placed both of his hands on his thighs, and handed over the controls by saying, "Yes Sir, you have the controls." The instructor and the student always exchanged these words to maintain a clear understanding of the pilot-in-command.

I sometimes vomited during flying, but continued pushing myself for the love of an adventurous career. My earlier flying instructors Flight Lieutenant Raashid Kalim and Flying Officer Mudassir supported my efforts. It was because of them that I continued flying despite landing with the vomit bag in my hand. Mudassir was soon to be posted out of Risalpur Academy to Air Base Mianwali.

I was assigned a new instructor pilot. My new instructor wasn't so kind. He called me a 'Sissy' -meaning a coward - during flying. Insulted by his unkind remark, I decided to check the courage of my instructor.

Putting the aircraft into a spin and recovering out of it was considered to be the most dangerous and nerve-wracking maneuvre by student pilots. This flight maneuvre was so risky that we were taught to eject out of the cockpit if the spin did not recover from above ten thousand feet.

The spin included a rotation of the entire aircraft from nose to tail axis combined with rapid fall towards the ground.

My new instructor thoroughly explained to me the procedure of entering and recovering from the spin during the preflight briefing on the ground. According to the preflight briefing, he was to put the aircraft into a spin and I was to quickly initiate the recovery procedure on hearing the command, "Recover, you have the controls."

After takeoff, we climbed to twenty thousand feet in the training area to enter the spin. At twenty thousand feet, he reduced the speed by bringing the throttle full back to the idle position and by gradually lifting the nose of the aircraft. He held on to the control stick with both hands till it started to buffet. The stall warning light flashed in the cockpit while I heard its beeping sound in my headset. He then kicked the right rudder with the force of his right leg and moved the control stick to the right from the full back position. The aircraft rotated after it dipped to the right and the spin fully stabilized after a couple of rotations. The aircraft, rotating to the right, started losing altitude rapidly as we held on tightly to our seats.

I took over the controls as soon as I heard the command,

**"Recover Sissy, you have the controls."**

Though unhappy with the remark, I replied,

"Yes Sir, I have the controls."

I did not initiate the spin-recovery procedure as briefed on the ground. Instead, I continued spinning by keeping the control stick back into my stomach with both hands and by maintaining pressure on the right rudder.

He again said,

"Recover."

This time without the word sissy, but I maintained the spin by keeping pressure on the controls.

He shouted,

"I have the controls!"

I ignored his command.

He shouted again and with panic this time,

"I have the controls!"

I kept my eyes on the altimeter, carefully watching the fast-declining altitude. As we were crossing fifteen thousand feet, I left the controls and replied, "Yes Sir, you have the controls." We heard each other breathing heavily through our oxygen masks. ˙

It was compulsory to eject if the spin did not recover by ten thousand feet above the ground. I took a calculated risk and gave him time to recover the aircraft long before reaching ten thousand feet. I also knew that I had given him a panic attack in checking his courage.

My instructor immediately recovered the aircraft out of the spin. He applied the opposite left rudder with the force of his left leg and pushed forward the stick with the full force of both his hands. The aircraft stopped rotating and recovered in a dive. He gradually pulled back the stick and added power as we leveled off above thirteen thousand feet.

My instructor turned my oxygen to 100 percent and turned the air-conditioning ducts towards my face by stretching his hand to my side of the control panel. He then said with an awkward accent, **"You are not a Sissy; you are an Idiot."**

In my opinion, that was an appropriate comment. I replied,

"Yes Sir," and smiled inside my oxygen mask.

# Broken Wings

There was an unwritten code in the academy - never, ever speak against your instructor. After some unhappy incidents, I went to my Flight Commander and humbly requested him to change my flying instructor. I accepted this unsuccessful match as my inability to follow his style of training without speaking a word against him. The Flight Commander listened to me and promised to do something. After some time he called me into his office. My instructor was already sitting there, waiting. The Flight Commander humiliated me and told me of breaking the code. This code had never before been broken in the history of the academy. A student pilot had never complained against his instructor pilot. Reduced to tears, I left the room of the Flight Commander with the guilt of breaching the academy code. Though I had been scheduled for a mission the next day, I was suspended from flying without even flying the usual check mission that was necessary for suspension.

I had learned all the basic fighter flying maneuvres before my wings were cut to join the ground branch of Air Traffic Control. My passion to enjoy an adventurous life vanished upon my suspension from flying. It was a deep cut at my heart like losing a loved one. I cried for hours in the solitude of my room. My coursemates shared the grief. My batman Ibrahim, a character, cried with me on hearing the news of my suspension.

**I moved on quickly, leaving the pain behind by promising myself always to remain a fighter pilot in my mind. This I did.**

After suspension from flying, I served the PAF with pride. Today, I continue to cherish the fond memories. You will notice in the coming pages that it has remained my priority to extract adventure out of every opportunity provided by life.

*Wing Cdr. Mudassir-My T-37 Flying Instructor*

*With Air Marshal Raashid Kalim--My MFI-17 Flying Instructor*

*Malik Hakim*

*Mushshak flying with the 3rd Supp G.D.(P) Course.*
*Instructors sitting from the Left:*
*Flt. Lt. Zahoor, Flt. Lt. Shabbir, Sqn. Ldr. Hameed, Flt. Lt. Ghafoor,*
*Flt. Lt. Asad, Flt. Lt. Raashid Kalim,*

*Standing First row:*
*Flt. Cdt. Kaleem, Flt. Cdt. Ali, Flt. Cdt. Mushtaq, Flt. Cdt. Rehman, Flt.*
*Cdt. Saqib, Flt. Cdt. Tariq, Flt. Cdt. Javed, Flt. Cdt. Liaquat,*
*Flt. Cdt. Shahid, Flt. Cdt. Alamgir, Flt. Cdt. Rahat,*

*Standing 2nd row:*
*Flt. Cdt. Amjad, Flt. Cdt. Nusrat, Flt. Cdt. Raza,*
*Flt. Cdt. Shahzad, Flt. Cdt. Maroof, Flt. Cdt. Waheed, Javed,*
*Flt. Cdt. Ahmed and Flt. Cdt. Attiya from Bahrain*

*From Left: Tubraz, Najam & Sikander*

*From Left: Sikander, Nusrat, Kazim and Ibrahim*

# Chapter Three

# Becoming an Air Traffic Control Officer

From the time it starts its engines before taxiing to the time it switches them off after landing, an aircraft always remains in radio contact with one or another Air Traffic Control (ATC) unit. Air traffic controllers behind the glass walls of the Control Towers are the only controllers who physically see the landings and takeoffs of the aircraft. The rest of the Air Traffic Control units maintain contact with the aircraft by means of radio communication or by observing them on their radar screens.

Air traffic controllers from the glass house Control Towers grant startup, taxiing, takeoff, and landing instructions. In addition, they also relay airfield weather, serviceability of radio navigational aids, or any other messages for the timely knowledge of the personnel involved in flight operations.

ATC towers control a limited area of a few nautical miles around the airfield that extends up to a few thousand feet. This area of control is called the Aerodrome Traffic Zone (ADZ). A nautical mile is slightly more than a statute mile in measure.

Immediately after leaving the aerodrome traffic zone, all aircraft switch to Approach Control frequency. Approach Controllers have a larger area of responsibility starting from outside the Aerodrome Control Zone, up to a horizontal defined distance in nautical miles, and vertically up from a few thousand feet to unlimited altitudes. This area is called the Approach Control Zone. Approach Controllers provide flight separation and Air Traffic information services to maintain an orderly flow of air traffic. Approach Controllers in general are equipped with radar and provide service by monitoring the aircraft on radar screens in the form of blips.

Air Traffic from the Approach Control is transferred to the Flight Information Region (FIR). This is a much larger high-level area of responsibility in the form of air corridors. FIR provides flight information services to all the aircraft flying through their respective areas.

After suspension from flying, I reported at Sargodha Air Base for On-The-Job Training (O.J.T.) as an Air Traffic Controller. Sargodha Air Base, located west of Lahore, housed No. 5 Squadron of Mirages, No. 11 Squadron of F-6s, and the prestigious squadron of Combat and Command School (CCS). It also housed the Headquarters of the Central Air Command. During the 1965 and 1971 wars with India, Sargodha was the nucleus of the Pakistan Air Force.

Air Commodore Daud Pota commanded the Sargodha Air Base. Wing Commander M.M.H. Rana acted as the Senior Air Traffic Control Officer (SATCO) commanding the ATC Squadron. Squadron Leader Sherwani was second in command of the ATC. The other ATC officers included Flight Lieutenant Anwar Qureshi, Flying Officer Shakeel Malik, and pilot officers Mian Ibad, Naeem Ghori, Mujahid Jafri, and Mahmood Sultan. It was a crowd of great fun-loving and professionally solid officers. Shakeel Malik earned our respect for his excellent professional abilities.

Flight Lieutenant Khalid Khawaja was our chief Air Traffic Control Instructor. He later left the Air Force and took an active part in the Afghan War against the Russians. Khalid Khawaja and Colonel Imam were later assassinated by the Taliban. Khawaja had a frank and courageous personality. I enjoyed many interesting discussions on religion with the late Sir Khalid Khawaja. My original course was 65th G.D.(P.). I remained away from flying due to participation in an inter-boxing competition in Karachi. Meanwhile my course was promoted to T-37 aircraft and I was relegated to complete flying with the 3rd supplementary course. After suspension from flying I joined the Air Traffic Controller's course with three other cadets who came from the 66th and the 4th Supplementary G.D.(P.) courses. As such, I earned the privilege of being the coursemate of 65th, 66th, 3rd, and 4th Supplementary courses.

For the ATC course, there were three other suspended flight cadets reduced to the status of cadet after suspension from flying. They were Cadet Masood Ahmed, Cadet Sajid Mumtaz, and Cadet Zafar Amin. Masood retired as a Squadron Leader and lives in Vancouver, Canada. Sajid retired from the service after rising to the rank of Air Commodore. Zafar left the Air Force as a Squadron Leader and joined the Civil Service. He served the cabinet division as a joint secretary. Finally, on the 7th of April, 1978, with three other coursemates, I was commissioned as Pilot Officer in the Air Traffic Control (A.T.C.) branch of the Air Force. It was a joyful day as Air Commodore Azeem Daud Pota, Base Commander of Sargodha Air Base, inserted the ranks of Pilot Officer on our shoulders in a simple ceremony held at the office of Wing Commander Rana at Sargodha Air Base. It may have been nothing compared to the grand passing out parade of my G.D.(P.) coursemates at Risalpur, but we were happy to be officers of the Air Force. Besides other privileges, we were also entitled to respond to the salutes from our juniors. We were posted out to four different ATC squadrons of the Air Force. I was posted to Masroor Air Base in Karachi.

# First Posting to Air Base Masroor

With the rank of Pilot Officer on my shoulders, the Air Force presented me with honour, respect, and freedom on a silver platter. Flying Officer Adil Rasheed, a dear buddy from my Satellite Town neighbourhood in Rawalpindi, received me when I reported to the officers' mess of Air Force Base Masroor in Karachi. Popularly known as 'Pir Adil', he was a couple of courses senior to me with all the traits of a carefree and fun-loving person. I always addressed him by his first name. At times, some of his coursemates raised an eyebrow at me for not using the word 'Sir' while addressing him, but most of them knew about our friendship. Credit for this frank relationship belonged to Adil. Despite being senior in the Air Force, he honoured the neighbourhood friendship over service protocol.

Adil, a rare character of his kind, was a pilot of No. 18 Squadron. He had arranged my room in the same No. 9 block of the officers' mess where seniors lived. We again lived together in the same building behind No. 4 block after getting married later in 1981. Our wives also got along well and we largely enjoyed our days at Masroor Air Base. Adil retired from the service after reaching the rank of Squadron Leader. He lives in Toronto with his family and continues to fly for different airlines of the world.

Masroor Air Base, built in 1940-1941 by the British Royal Indian Air Force (RIAF), became Royal Pakistan Air Force (RPAF) station Mauripur when Pakistan came into being on the 14th of August, 1947. Located close to the shores of the Indian Ocean, near the famous beach of Hawke's Bay, it was later named the Pakistan Air Force (PAF) Base Mauripur. A former Base Commander, Air Commodore Masroor Hussain crashed in June 1967 after his bomber collided with a bird. He managed to direct the burning aircraft away from a populated area before crashing. The base was renamed PAF Base Masroor in honour of the former Base Commander. In April 1978 when I first reported, Air Commodore Nawabzada Rehmatullah commanded the Masroor Base. He was the father of TV celebrity star Marina Khan. Group Captain Aziz acted as Officer Commanding Flying Wing. Group Captain Siddiqui was the OC Admin Wing and Wing Commander Sitara Yousaf was the Senior Medical Officer (SMO). PAF Base Masroor housed No. 32 Tactical Attack Wing.

Wing Commander Mushtaq Laghari commanded the No. 18 Squadron. He was a well-liked commanding officer. Broad chest, stout physique, intelligent eyes, and a heavy moustache were the hallmarks of the graceful personality of Wing Commander Laghari.

The American T-33, popularly known as the T-bird, belonged to No. 2 Squadron that performed as a fighter conversion unit (FCU) for the newly graduated pilots from Risalpur. The squadron also carried a couple of reconnaissance aircraft. Wing Commander Tanvir Afghan commanded No. 2 Squadron.

Wing Commander Mazhar commanded the B-57 bombers of No. 7 Squadron and Wing Commander Umar was the OC Rescue Squadron of H-43 Husky helicopters.

Wing Commander T.R. Khan, Senior Air Traffic Control Officer (SATCO), controlled the Air Traffic Control Squadron. He was a good, professional air traffic controller who was liked by his subordinates. T.R. was known as an officer with a strong personality.

Soon the command at the base would change. Air Commodore Waqar Azim took over as Base Commander. Short, fair, grey-haired, and handsome - the man was considered a terror on the base. Group Captain Dilawar came in as Officer Commanding the flying wing. He was a fatherly figure with the calm face of a true commander.

Wing Commander Rana soon replaced Wing Commander T. R. Khan as the SATCO. All the commanders at the base were thoroughly professional officers. Wing Commander Rana was a hard taskmaster. He worked hard and demanded the maximum effort from his subordinates.

## Establishing the Rani Garden

One day, while inspecting the taxi tracks from his car Base Commander, Waqar Azim radioed for SATCO Rana to report to him on the taxi track. Overgrown bushes around a large area opposite the Control Tower created a flight safety hazard that extended behind the tarmac for the helicopters to an area all along the two taxi tracks leading towards runway 09 from the bomber and T-bird tarmac. Air Commodore Azim tasked Wing Commander Rana to clear the entire area. Wing Commander Rana ordered us to supervise the bush-clearing operation out in the sun. This became detestably hard work for the elegant ATC officers who were accustomed to controlling traffic while sipping tea from within an air-conditioned glasshouse.

We performed the supervisory duties by taking hour-long turns, but none of us liked the unpleasant task. Military life does not allow the privilege of refusing orders. It became even more impossible to object when we saw that Wing Commander Rana himself was taking an hourly turn in the sun. The project needed a vast area cleared. It would not be possible to complete this clearing within a few months, considering the limited force of about twenty civilian workers equipped with only long blade machetes.

During this clearing project, two naval helicopters crashed in midair over Air Base Faisal a few miles from Masroor. Wing Commander Rana was named a member of the investigating team. The inquiry would keep him away from the taxi track-clearing operation as it was regarded as an award-winning challenge. Some officers remarked that the Squadron Commanders at the base were in competition for Sitara-e-Basalat, a military award granted for outstanding service at the rank of Wing Commander.

We had a great team of ATC officers headed by Flight Lieutenant Khalid Khawaja that included Flight Lieutenant Shamsher, Flying Officer Sabir, Flying Officer Moazzam, Flying Officer Khattak, and Pilot Officer Azhar. I was the most junior officer with a few months of commissioned service behind me. Rana was aware of the non-cooperative attitude of all the officers. Before leaving for the inquiry, he called me to his office. Sadness and disappointment were evident in his face as he spoke with pain in his voice.

Then he asked me to take charge of the clearing operation during his absence. This was more of a request and less of an order. I must admit that the histrionics of Rana touched my heart and inspired me to devote all my energy to the job.

I went to my room and tried to figure out a better way to perform the bush-clearing operation. I thought of the army engineering unit that had been deployed to re-carpet the runway surface. Captain Naveed from the Pakistan Army was the officer in charge. I enjoyed good terms with him as we often shared views during lunch time at the dinning hall.

I had seen many bulldozers placed on the non-active side of the runway. I took my idea to Captain Naveed. He at once assigned the job to one of his soldiers who operated a heavy bulldozer with about an eight-foot by three-foot blade attached to the front of the machine. I briefed the driver about the operation and left him with our team of workers to help out. I ordered lunch for the driver from the officers' mess at my own expense and returned to my room.

After a few hours, I drove to the location in the jeep that had been placed at my disposal by Wing Commander Rana. My heart leapt with joy as I saw the entire area cleared of bushes. The whole area looked as clean and brown as a fresh cricket field. The clearing operation, expected to take months with the available civilian work force, had been completed in a few hours. I am not sure why no one else had figured out this solution before. Perhaps my friendship with Captain Naveed had allowed me to speculate.

My success made me the golden boy of Wing Commander Rana, and he handed me the administrative task of decorating the air field. Life became wonderful, as I was provided with a staff car to arrange flowers from civilian sources outside the air force base. I visited the Director of Horticulture at the Zoological Gardens in Karachi and asked for help. Mr. Hanif, a fine gentleman in his early fifties, was gracious enough to visit our site. Not only did he give me a plan, but he also supplied the potted flowers and truckloads of soil needed for the landscaping. ATC officers secretly named the area Rani Garden referring to Wing Commander Rana. Rani in Urdu language means a queen. The civil authorities provided all the material as a gift to the Air Force.

Wing Commander Rana received loads of appreciation from the Base Commander for completing the project. When it came time to write my Annual Confidential Report (ACR), Rana called me to his office. He looked into my eyes and said,

"Pilot Officer Nusrat, you are an asset to the Air Force. I have written a very good report for you. Very few officers at the start of their career get such a report."

Getting a good report was not my priority, and our relations were to worsen after that excellent report. In my opinion at that time, whatever good Rana did in service of the Air Force was driven by motivation for self promotion more than encouragement of the service. Getting a good report from Rana was considered a demerit by my emotional and immature mind. However, today, after thirty-eight years, I do not agree with my previous opinion. Wing Commander Rana was a hard-working disciplined officer. He rose to the rank of Group Captain before retiring from service.

There was plenty of life beyond the Control Tower. Flying Officer Adil, my best buddy on the base, always planned our evenings and we visited all the delicious food places around town. Two civilian friends, Afzal Khan and Ejaz Rasheed, joined us on our outings. Afzal was a good singer; he arranged a group of musicians. Many other officers of the block joined our late night gatherings. Flying Officers S. T. Chaudhry, Nawaz Khattak, Waliullah Khokar, Javed Burki, and many others were regular partners in our escapades.

The billiards room in the officers' mess was our favourite place to pass the time. We played billiards all night, betting over delicious shami kebabs and chicken tikka of the mess. Life was full of fun and laughter.

*Adil, Nusrat, Iftikhar and Mian Ayub*

*Sohail and Nusrat*

*Yawar, Saqib, Alamgir and Shahid*

# Chapter Four
## The Battles of Cherat

In 1980, I was promoted to the rank of Flying Officer and posted to Cherat, a beautiful hill station at an elevation of 4,500 feet about thirty miles from Peshawar. The 'Khattak Bus' was the only mode of regular civil transport available at Cherat. It arrived and left the same day. Pubbi, on the main GT road about fifteen miles down the hills, was the other access point to catch any other transport. The 'Khattak Bus' dictated arrival and departure times from Cherat.

The Cherat cantonment, a well-guarded, gated community controlled by the Pakistan Army, was a training centre for the Commandos of the Special Services Group (SSG). Commandos of the Pakistan Army were a different breed. Most of them were passionate and dedicated souls with a carefree attitude towards life. The mountains around Cherat always echoed with the laughter of these brave and lively officers. I enjoyed good terms with most of the Commandos.

The Air Force had a small setup of No. 411 Squadron of the Air Defence Weapon Corps (ADWC). No. 213 Flight of Air Traffic Control (ATC) also formed part of the same squadron. Air Base Peshawar looked after the administrative needs of the Air Force personnel posted at Cherat.

SQN. LDR. Nusrat Hussain (R)

# From the Cockpit of a Jumbo-747 Aircraft

Cherat Approach Control was the most complex station that I ever worked at over my entire Air Traffic Control service. Islamabad, Dhamial, Kamra, Risalpur, and Peshawar were the five aerodromes located within the Cherat Control Zone. Area of control extended from ground to an unlimited altitude with a sixty nautical mile radius centred at Attock Bridge. All domestic and international commercial flights flying in and out of Peshawar and Islamabad soared though this area. In addition, the Air Force fighter aircraft and army helicopters and light aircraft also conducted their exercises within the same airspace. The Approach Control was not equipped with radar facilities. Air traffic was controlled by listening to the reported position of the aircraft. Controllers formed a mental picture of all the aircraft and provided separation by marking their positions on paper strips placed in front of them. The Control Zone of sixty nautical miles in rush hour was filled with all types of aircraft ranging from low-level flying helicopters of the army to the subsonic and supersonic fighter aircraft of the Air Force. Medium body and wide body domestic and international commercial flights comprised of Fokker to Jumbo aircraft also transited through the same airspace. I remember singlehandedly controlling several types of thirty-seven aircraft operating at the same time on two different radios of VHF (Very High Frequency) and UHF (Ultra High Frequency) under my control. This extraordinary station allowed controllers to gain tremendous confidence in their controlling abilities.

Flight Lieutenant Sulaiman Yaseen was SATCO. He was a sweet soul and my immediate boss at Cherat. One weekend, I went to my parents' home in Islamabad which was a few hours' drive from Cherat. My wife, Shaheen, was my fiancée then. She lived in Karachi with her parents. When I talked to her by telephone from Islamabad, she enquired about my plan of visiting Karachi. I bragged to her that I would reach there the next day if she asked me to come. She knew that I was to report to Cherat the next day and that it wasn't possible to reach Karachi so soon. I had always considered her to be rational and was confident that she would not put me to the test. However, to my surprise, she asked me to visit her the next day. She called my bluff. Being a love-struck young boy and an officer of the Air Force, it became a matter of honouring my words. Yet I was also certain the Air Force wouldn't consider it a matter of honour if I asked for leave under the pretext of seeing my fiancée.

My adventurous mind presented a perfect plan to honour the words of an Air Force Officer and a lover boy. The next day, I boarded a Pakistan International Airlines Jumbo-747 flight from Islamabad to Karachi at the same time I was to board a bus for duty at Cherat.

Because of my experience, I was aware the flight I was boarding would contact my workplace immediately after takeoff. It would remain in contact with Cherat Approach for ten to twelve minutes; therefore, as soon as I boarded the plane, I introduced myself to the air hostess and asked her to deliver immediately a note to the captain of the aircraft that read:

"Dear Captain,

Sir—please ask my SATCO, Flight Lieutenant Sulaiman Yaseen at Cherat Approach Control, to approve my ten days of emergency leave. I am on board your aircraft, and I am your Air Traffic Controller at Cherat Approach.

Flying Officer Nusrat Hussain"

A few minutes after takeoff, the air hostess told me the captain wanted to see me in the cockpit. I was expecting his summons because I knew that my boss at Cherat would want to hear from me.

The captain asked me to take the jump seat in the cockpit of the Jumbo-747 and gave me the headset to speak with the SATCO on manual frequency. After occupying the jump seat and adjusting the headset, I transmitted on manual frequency to Cherat,

"Cherat Approach control, this is Flying Officer Nusrat from Pakistan 301."

I heard the sweet voice of the SATCO over the headset. He inquired,

"Yes Nusrat— what is it?"

I replied with a humble tone,

"Sir—I had to go to Karachi to attend to an emergency. Please approve my leave for ten days."

There were a few moments of silence on the radio, and then came the sweet voice of the SATCO:

"Ok Nusrat, but come back after ten days."

"Yes, Sir— and thank you very much!" I replied and headed back to my seat after thanking the captain and his first officer in the cockpit.

Flight Lieutenant Khursheed Mirza, a dear friend of mine, was sitting in the Approach office at that time. He later told me that after approving my leave, the SATCO had said,

"How could I refuse when he was already in the aircraft climbing to thirty-three thousand feet?"

On my return to duty, the SATCO wanted to know the emergency. He called me to his office and asked in a serious tone,

"Flying Officer Nusrat - so let us hear what exactly the emergency was."

There was obviously no emergency response in my book that could have satisfied his latter line of questions. I replied by almost bringing tears to my eyes,

"Sir—I am thankful that you approved my leave, but please do not ask me again about the nature of my emergency. Sir, I cannot disclose a very personal family matter to anyone."

His expression revealed that he had uttered a four-letter word for me in his mind. But he smiled generously, winked, and said,

"Okay— carry on, young man."

The generous Commander knowingly ignored my naughty behaviour.

# Fist Fight for Pride

Major Zafar was the most senior bachelor officer in Cherat acting as Deputy Assistant Adjutant and Quartermaster General, in short called the DQ. His room, which was close to mine, often provided opportunity for candid discussions on various matters of common interest. One night we ended up in a heated discussion. I never meant to insult the Special Services Group (SSG) as an institution, but he considered some of my words as derogatory remarks for the SSG. This incident created a rift between us.

Major Zafar felt insulted and told Major Kamal Shaukat who was a much more passionate officer of the SSG. Being emotional and sensitive to the pride of the SSG, Kamal was offended to hear the words coming from a 'Sissy' - a name given to the Air Force officers by the army Commandos. One late night, Major Kamal, along with Captain Amir and Captain Arshad, came to my room to seek an explanation for my derogatory remarks about the SSG.

I tried to explain that I had never meant to talk badly about the SSG as a formation. Major Kamal recounted the rich history of the SSG, a formation dearer than life to him. In the heat of discussion, he grabbed me by the collar and threatened grave consequences. Flight Lieutenant Khursheed Mirza from the adjoining area, after listening to the noise, came into my room. On his intervention, all three left angrily.

Major Kamal was about six feet tall with the solid build of a Commando. Frankly speaking, fear overtook my courage in the presence of the three army commandos. Panic stopped me from reacting when he grabbed my collar. I had always thought myself to be a brave man, but that night I chickened out - I admit.

If reported to higher authorities, then the three of them would be punished for trespassing and assaulting. I was an emotional Flying Officer, not interested in getting them punished by the military. I wanted to get even with the commandos' mentality who considered the Air Force officers to be sissies. Major Kamal was the only one who used harsh language and grabbed me by the collar. The other two officers remained silent throughout the conflict. I couldn't react because of my terror of the three Commandos. The insult of not reacting haunted me. It became a matter of pride of the Air Force. I did not sleep that night and stayed awake, thinking.

Kamal was about six feet tall and had the strong build of a commando. He was stronger and taller than my five feet seven inches. As I thought of my boxing abilities, the words of my boxing coach, Chief Tech Yaqub, echoed in my mind: "Always stay closer while fighting a tall person to neutralize the full force of his punch." I had once knocked out a taller opponent following the same rule. I gathered my confidence. Like Shakespeare's tragic hero, I decided to challenge Major Kamal to a duel to restore my personal dignity and the pride of my organization as well.

The next day when Major Kamal walked up the road after the morning parade, I stopped him and politely invited him to my room. He looked tired and sweaty after the parade. Signs of worry from last night's action were also clear on his face. He silently followed me. I locked the door as soon as he sat on the chair inside my room. He looked nervous but overcame his nervousness with a friendly smile. I offered two choices in response to his behaviour from the previous night. First, a duel following the boxing rules until one of us bled or asked to stop the fight. Second, I would report the matter to the Air Force authorities.

He was aware of the consequences if reported: a joint investigation by the Army and the Air Force leading to a court-martial. My proposal brought some relief to his face. He chose the first option and asked for a few days before the fight. I unlocked the door and he left with the promise to respond soon.

We continued with our normal routine. After a few days, while watching TV in the ante-room, he asked me if I still wanted to fight. I responded, "The sooner the better." He appeared ready and walked to my room. I locked the door, moved the bed to a corner to create space for fighting, and reminded him of the boxing rules as we took off our wristwatches and placed them on the table.

We stood facing each other with our bare fists clenched tightly in boxing style. I fought close to his body, when I suddenly got his punch breaking my defence straight on my lips. My mouth tasted blood. I knew that I was bleeding, when suddenly I got the chance to throw a right hook below his left eye. He sighed loudly in pain. I saw his skin popping up and turning blue. I was even. I immediately called off the fight. It hadn't lasted more than a few minutes. We shook hands and hugged each other. A strange bond of respect was formed between us that night. Major Kamal in appreciation said, "I wish you were in SSG with us." I had once again managed to change the Sissy impression, and this time it had happened by restoring the Air Force pride as a fighting arm. No Sissy.

The next day, when I met Major Kamal in the mess, I noticed the blue mark under his left eye. My swollen lip was obvious. We smiled, carefully viewing each other's faces. Major Kamal Shaukat later retired as a Brigadier.

# First Summary of Evidence

I always found it interesting to confront my superior officers whenever I found them using their command illegally or unfairly. Officer Commanding (OC) Cherat, known for liberally ordering

Summary of Evidence, developed a dislike towards me for my obvious carefree attitude. I was a Flying Officer and the OC was a Squadron Leader from the Air Defence Weapons Corps with insufficient knowledge about the operational duty of Air Traffic Control. He once asked me to leave my place of duty and report to his office. I was the only controller on duty and flying was in progress. I tried to explain that I cannot leave while flying is in progress, but he was insitant that I comply with his order. I was well aware of my operational duty and of my right to refuse his illegal command. I refused. This was the beginning of our unhealthy relationship.

A commissioned officer could only receive a punishment if a Summary of Evidence proved him guilty. A senior officer records an investigation and it is sent to the Legal Directorate of the Air Headquarters for recommendation. Depending on the findings, the Legal branch either dismisses or recommends a summary trial by an officer of a higher rank. A reprimand or severe reprimand awarded by summary disposal remains un-challengeable by the accused officer. However, a serious punishment amounting to loss of seniority or more allows the aggrieved officer to seek a retrial by a court-martial.

One weekend I went out to Islamabad from Cherat and fell sick with fever. There were three different Military Hospitals around Rawalpindi and Islamabad at that time: The Air Force Hospital at Chaklala, The Combined Military Hospital (C.M.H.), and The Military Hospital (M.H.). These hospitals were available to provide medical facilities to the personnel of all three forces.

Upon reporting sick at the Air Force Hospital Chaklala, the doctor advised me Excused Duty (E.D.) for three days. According to the Air Force laws, E.D. requires complete rest and forbids a person from going out of his room. In my case, the law prohibited me from travelling to Cherat.

I informed Cherat about the E.D. The OC ordered me to report to the squadron and rest in my room at Cherat. His command was unlawful: I knew it, and the OC knew it as well. I refused to return and stayed in my home in Islamabad.

After three days I recovered, but naughtily went again to see a different doctor to the Combined Military Hospital this time. This doctor had no knowledge of my earlier sick report from the Air Force hospital. He too gave me E.D. for three days. I again told Cherat about the E.D. for another three days. The OC again ordered me to return to Cherat and rest in my room. Again, I refused and stayed home.

Both of us were well aware of our actions - he, for issuing an illegal order, and I, for my lawful right. He was entitled to ask, but I had the right to refuse.

I wanted to prolong the game further. After six days of E.D.'s, I went to a third doctor at the Military Hospital (M.H.) in Rawalpindi and managed another three days E.D. from him. I again informed Cherat about E.D. for three further days. This time, the OC did not ask me to return to Cherat.

Besides giving E.D. letters to me, the hospitals also sent signals directly to my squadron, officially telling them about the off-duty status of their officer.

When I had told my unit in Cherat about the E.D., they had also received two signals originating from the Air Force Hospital and the C.M.H. The M.H. did not send a signal for some unknown reason. However, the official record of my E.D. was available at the hospital.

The official signal of my last three days on E.D. from the M.H. did not reach them in Cherat. Therefore, they checked my status of last three days from the Air Force and the Combined Military Hospitals. They could not trace the last three days of E.D. at either hospital. It obviously wasn't there, as I had taken the third set of E.D.'s from the M.H.

They did not bother to check with the M.H. The OC believed that I had lied about my last three days of E.D. I did not clarify about my last visit to the M.H. Instead, I played the game, letting them grow stronger in their belief.

On reporting at duty, Fltight Lieutenant Gohar Javed, who was SATCO at the time, asked me to provide the E.D. letters issued by the hospital- the OC wanted to see them. I told him that they were in my room and I would hand them over the next day.

When asked the next day, I told him I had forgotten that the papers were in my home at Islamabad. I even asked for leave of one day to get them back from Islamabad. He ignored my request without asking any further questions.

The OC thought that he had a monkey with his hands in the cookie jar. He immediately ordered his staff officer to record a Summary of Evidence against me. Base Routine Orders (BROs) published Flight Lieutenant Gohar Javed as the summary recording officer. A signal about the summary was also sent to the Peshawar Air Force Base and the Legal Directorate.

I was under the constant legal advice of Flying Officer Danish, a lawyer and my favourite junior at Lower Topa from our cadetship days. He then served the Legal Directorate of the Air Force. He assured me 'No harm' under the prevailing evidence.

On the date of recording the summary, I stood before Flight Lieutenant Gohar Javed, the summary recording officer. For me, it was a scene of a comedy movie. My good friends worried about my career. I was charged with 'Absent without Leave' for three days and for telling lies about the E.D. report. If proven guilty, those charges could remove me from service.

Flying Officer Bangash, the Base Adjutant, confirmed that he had checked my medical record at the Air Force Hospital, Chaklala, and the C.M.H. Rawalpindi. He also confirmed that the record of the last three days of E.D. was not available at the Air Force Hospital, nor was it available at the C.M.H. I asked him,

"Did you check my E.D. from the Military Hospital, the M.H. in Rawalpindi?"

He responded,

"No, I did not check the Military Hospital, the M.H. in Rawalpindi."

I thanked him by saying,

"No further questions, please."

I took out the official papers of E.D. from my pocket and recorded my statement:

"I had repeatedly informed the higher authorities that I was on E.D. for all the days charged for absence. I now produce the excused duty papers of all the nine days issued by the doctors of the PAF, the C.M.H., and the M.H. hospitals."

Flight Lieutenant Gohar, the summary recording officer, looked at me in surprise with an open mouth. He then carefully looked at the papers for his satisfaction and attached them to the record of the summary.

The legal branch at the Air Headquarters dismissed the summary. The exercise of recording the summary had gone against them. For me it proved a learning experience of recording a Summary of Evidence without any risk or prejudice to my service.

# Summaries of Evidence-'Two in One'

A day before the Eid holidays, I was on afternoon duty when an army helicopter airborne from Risalpur headed to Army Aviation Base Dhamial, which is situated close to my home town of Islamabad. My ground position at Cherat was about 15 minutes away from the route of the helicopter. When the helicopter pilot came in my area of control and made radio contact, I asked if it would be possible for him to pick me up from Cherat. Considering the Eid holidays, the kind pilot agreed and diverted to pick me up from Cherat.

Flying Officer Sattar, the other controller, was to relieve me from duty after half an hour. There wasn't an aircraft in the air at that time and no other flight except the helicopter was scheduled for the next hour. I took all the required actions of informing the concerned agencies about the helicopter diversion to Cherat. I had also trained the other ranks of the ATC to handle light traffic in case of an emergeny. I then briefed the Chief Tech on duty with me in the Ops Room to handle this single helicopter until the arrival of Flying Officer Sattar. I had taken a calculated risk of leaving my place of duty.

However, as per standing operational orders, Air Traffic Controllers must change duty only after a proper handover to the next qualified controller. The OC came to know about the lapse in change of my duty. He ordered that a Summary of Evidence be recorded against me. He was sure that he had the monkey with hands in the cookie jar this time.

I must admit in all honesty that with the help of Flying Officer Zahid Bangash and Flight Lieutenant Khusrsheed Mirza, we tampered with the timings of my departure before sending the summary to the Legal Directorate of the Air Force. Therefore, the summary was again turned down by the Legal Directorate. This outcome surprised and further anguished the OC.

It so happened that after rejection of the Summary of Evidence by the Legal Directorate, the Air Force announced its annual exercise 'Jet Stream'. Air Headquarters attached me to the exercise on temporary duty to Air Base Masroor. After the exercise, my wedding would take place in Karachi. I applied for one month annual leave after the expiry of temporary duty from Masroor. Air Headquarters approved my annual leave after the exercise.

Air Commodore Salim then commanded the Peshawar Air Base. He was aware of our rift at Cherat. Despite the rejection of the helicopter summary by the Legal Directorate, he decided to test the summary and ordered a date for me, during my annual leave, to appear before him at Peshawar Air Base for a summary trial.

I started my annual leave after completing the exercise duty at Air Base Masroor. Flying Officer Zahid Bangash, the base adjutant Cherat, told me by phone to appear on the ordered date before the Base Commander, Peshawar for the summary trial. The trial date was set on the thirteenth day of my thirty-day annual leave. I confirmed I would attend.

A few days before the hearing, I met with a road accident on a motorbike in Karachi and was admitted to hospital with my new bride. I could not travel and appear on the prescribed date of the trial. The Air Force hospital and I informed the authorities at Cherat. They did not cancel my annual leave and they did not tell me of any other action.

I was clear in my mind that I was to report for duty after enjoying the remaining seventeen days of the annual leave. When I reported at Cherat after my annual leave, to my surprise the OC ordered another Summary of Evidence. He charged me with seventeen days of absence without official leave. This charge shocked me. Seventeen days of absence by an officer, if proven, was a case of sure dismissal from the service.

I faced two summaries now: One - the helicopter airlift. Two - seventeen days of absence without official leave (AWOL).

Air Commodore Salim was posted out, and Air Commodore Nazir Jilani took over the command at Air Base Peshawar. Jilani was informed about my previous history - he became aware of the weakness of the earlier helicopter summary, so he dismissed the helicopter summary.

Instead of recording the new summary of the absence of seventeen days in Cherat, he decided to directly trial the charge at Air Base Peshawar. I consulted my pal, Flying Officer Danish in the Legal Directorate. He guided me through the cross-questions and again assured me of the harmlessness of the charges framed against me. He advised me to accept the light penalty of a reprimand or a severe reprimand. He also advised me to exercise my right of opting for court-martial if awarded the higher punishment of loss of seniority.

On the day of the trial, an officer escorted me in front of Air Commodore Jilani. He sat there with a serious expression in his ceremonial uniform wearing the gold braided silk peaked cap. I saluted the president by coming to the attention position because I did not wear my cap and steel belt with the uniform.

The law forbade the accused from wearing his uniform steel belt during the trial. The story goes that once, after hearing his punishment, an officer had taken out his belt to beat the sentence awarding officer. A later act included in the law stated that all the affirmed officers were to appear without wearing their steel belt before the court. I looked around in interest. It was a perfect setting of a courtroom. A clerk with his typewriter sat on a side of the Base Commander, constantly recording the proceedings.

I refused to plead guilty when the Base Commander read out the charge to me. They had charged me with an absence of seventeen days without official leave (AWOL). The Base Adjutant, Flying Officer Bangash, appeared as the first witness. He identified the accused (me) and stated that I had confirmed and agreed to appear for the helicopter summary trial on the prescribed date. I did not cross-question him.

OC Cherat appeared as the second witness. He stated to the court that the accused (me) had been told to attend the helicopter summary trial on the thirteenth day of his leave. He added that his leave of a further seventeen days had therefore been cancelled. I asked the court's permission to cross-examine my

Officer Commanding (OC). Air Commodore Nazir Jilani allowed this with a serious nod.

I asked Air Commodore Jilani,

"Sir, it is very difficult to cross-examine in the attention position. Can I come to at ease position, please?"

He looked into my eyes seriously and again granted permission with a nod of his head. I stretched my legs, put my right hand beside my right hip-joint, and looked towards the OC with a tilt of my head. He stood at the attention position looking straight towards Air Commodore Jilani. I heard the commanding voice of Air Commodore Jilani. He warned me,

"Flying Officer Nusrat, you were told to come to at ease position."

I immediately withdrew my right hand to cross with the left hand at my back and reached the proper at ease position.

At the same time I looked towards Air Commodore Jilani and said,

"Sorry, Sir."

Maintaining proper at ease position, I turned my face towards the OC. It was a rare sight for me—the OC in attention position and me at ease. I took a moment to enjoy it and then asked sharply,

"How was my annual leave cancelled when it was approved by the Air Headquarters?"

The OC did not look towards me; instead, he kept looking straight towards the president by upholding his attention position. He replied,

"I gave you only thirteen days of leave."

That was not true. I asked with venom in my voice,

"Do you know that as the OC you can only grant a leave of ten days? Under what authority did you grant me leave for thirteen days?"

I noticed the sweat appearing on his face. He repeated with the words fumbling out of his mouth, "I only gave you thirteen days of leave."

I did not ask any further questions and stated that I had gone on my annual leave that had been approved by the Air Headquarters. During the leave, I was to appear for the trial of helicopter summary before the Peshawer Base commander on the thirteenth day of my annual leave of thirty days. On that day I was in the hospital. The Air Force Hospital had officially informed Cherat of this circumstance. I had also informed the Base Adjutant. The OC had not given any further instructions, nor had he cancelled my leave. Air Headquarters, the leave approving authority, had not been told about canceling the leave. Therefore, after thirty days and the expiry of my annual leave, I had reported in time at my place of duty. I logically disproved the charge. The OC had nothing to state further so he was dismissed out of the room. I returned to my attention position. Air Commodore Jilani looked at me seriously and spoke before writing the judgment,

"I know the charge was not proven, but I also know there is something wrong with you too. Your OC gave you a leave of thirteen days. You had the guts to challenge his authority."

He took a pause and then announced,

"Considering limited experience in the service, I am awarding you reprimand."

He closed the case. A reprimand acted as a warning on the file, but did not carry any serious demerit. He asked me to wait outside his office.

The OC and I again appeared before the Base Commander. He asked us to sit down and said,

"I am putting both of you under observation for six months and would like you to behave in the future."

He kept his eyes on me while talking, but a warning for the OC was clearly evident within his command.

On my return to Cherat, I told my buddy officers that the OC was under observation by the Base Commander. We laughed about the whole episode.

After having the 'under observation' warning by the Base Commander, the OC and I disengaged and honourably withdrew from that nasty battlefield of Cherat.

I do not think the OC lied about cancelling my leave. He genuinely thought that the leave was cancelled. In his innocent opinion the leave was cancelled when I was ordered to report before summary trial on the thirteenth day of my leave. He believed himself to be a good commander and he believed me to be an evil officer. His desire of catching me with my hands in the cookie jar though, remained in his mind.

## Getting Married

I don't know why, but my life had always been in turbulence. Smooth sailing wasn't a part of my existence. Further turbulence took place at the time of my marriage, too.

Major Syed Zameer Jafri, the famous poet of Pakistan; Major Raees ud-din KhanSherani; and my father were close friends. They had served together as civilian clerks at the General Headquarters (G.H.Q.) of the Royal British Army in Shimla before the partition of India. Major Jafri and Major Sherani had joined the fighting arm while my father had continued serving in a civil capacity. After retirement from the army, Major Jafri joined the Capital Development Authority (CDA) and Major Sherani went to serve the Pakistan International Airlines. My father acted as Assistant Director in the CDA under his old friend Major Jafri. It is interesting to mention that Imtinan Zameer, son of Major Zameer Jafri, was my class fellow in the Central Government Model School of Satellite Town of Rawalpindi. We also bonded well in friendship; as such, our friendship travelled to the second generation. Imtinan lives in New York now and we maintain regular contact. Major General Ehtesham Zameer, elder son of Major Jaffery, also attended our school before joining the Military College Jehlum.

Brigadier Hatif selected my father to perform as Director of the Islamabad Sports Complex in Karachi. Brigadier Hatif, the famous chief of the Hockey Federation in Pakistan, acted as the Director General of the Islamabad Sports Complex. After posting to Karachi, my father lived close to the house of Major Sherani in P.E.C.H. Society. The families of the two old friends often visited each other.

During the same period of 1978, after my commission as a Pilot Officer, the Air Force posted me to Air Base Masroor in Karachi. My mother searched eagerly for my potential bride and she eventually chose a daughter of Major Sherani. I visited Major Sherani's house with my mother to look at my future wife. I liked Shaheen at first sight. She was beautiful and sober. Our parents launched the proposal. We started talking by phone. We liked each other and looked forward to a smooth marriage.

After retirement, my father moved back to Rawalpindi and later the Air Force posted me out to Cherat. Some misunderstandings erupted between our two families. They adopted a firm stance against one another on some issue. This risked our future marriage that had previously been agreed upon by the two families. Without giving importance to the emotions of the two people getting married, they mutually called off the wedding. They did not even bother to consult us before making their decision.

I tried to talk to my parents, but they had already decided my fate and were not interested in having any conversation on the subject. Shaheen, despite her desire to get married to me, was in no position to advance any dialogue on the topic. Cruel social values of our culture kicked in. I decided to have a soldier to soldier conversation with Major Sherani, father of Shaheen.

I took leave and went to see Major Sherani in Karachi. I asked him to reconsider his decision. He repeated similar complaints I had heard earlier from my family. An interesting conversation took place between me and Major Sherani. I thought of speaking the stark truth and politely told him, "Sir, I hope you are aware of the interests of your daughter."

He looked at me sharply, got up from his seat, took a deep breath, and added,

"Yes, I know it involves my daughter. I also know that getting her married to you or not getting her married to you is an evil either way. But, I have chosen the lesser evil by not getting her married to you."

I saw our love story coming to an end when my friends Syed Mohsin Raza Rizvi, S.T. Chaudhry, Ejaz Rasheed, Afzal Khan, Imran Khan Bangash, Nayyer Iqbal, Faheem Khan, Khalid Mirza, Nayyer Hasan, Captain Masna and a few others encouraged me to continue with my efforts. It is because of the help of my friends and the prayers of my wife that our families finally agreed to our marriage.

As long as he lived, I enjoyed the best friendly relations with my father-in-law, Major Sherani. I listened to his military stories with interest. I was with him in Karachi when he breathed his last, gave him the final bath with my hands, and laid down his body in the grave. My wife earned an obedient and a loving position with my parents. God gifted us with four children, Maheen, Mohammed, Mohib and Mahvish. Maheen is married to Waqar Saeed and lives in London. All of them are settled with reasonably decent jobs. Everyone has to receive his or her own share of blessings and challenges presented by life. All marriages are a mystery. Mine is no different, even after thirty-five long years.

*Abboo Saheb (left ) my father in law extreme right*

*Shaheen in the middle with her mother and my mother.*

*My friends at the wedding*

*From Left: Afzal, Amer, Bangash Nusrat,*
*Ejaz, Maula and Sohail (sitting).*

*Khurshid Mirza, Nusrat and Shaheen at Cherat catchment area.*

*Nusrat, Khattak, Ali and Wali in front of Cherat BOQ's.*

# Chapter Five
## ATC Course in Hyderabad

Excitement and joy filled my heart upon receiving the signal from Air Headquarters to attend the Civil ATC course. An opportunity of ultimate freedom from the disciplined environment of the Air Force had arrived. The signal mentioned the names of nine other Flight Lieutenants with around four years of service to attend the course. All the officers, known to each other from our previous days, reported together at the Civil Aviation Training Institute (CATI) in Hyderabad.

Opposite the airport, on the banks of the Indus River in Hyderabad, there stood the impressive compound of CATI buildings. These buildings housed the training rooms and expensive equipment provided by the International Civil Aviation Organization (ICAO). ICAO formed a part of the United Nations Organization with its Headquarters in Montreal, Canada. Officers' living quarters and a dining hall were equally compatible with the modern officers' messes of the Air Force. The complex also housed a separate building for training the firefighters and carried up-to-date crash tenders and fire training equipment.

Flight Lieutenant Farooq Janjua, popularly known as 'Janj', was the most senior officer and I happened to be the most junior. Janj, a man of great qualities, possessed the talents of a lovable commander. Throughout our stay at CATI the ten Air Force officers jelled together as a great team, thanks to his leadership qualities. Janj later joined the Department of Civil Aviation. He had gone for the categorization test of the Civilian Controllers in Faisalabad when he died of a heart attack in his hotel room. May the Almighty bless his soul in paradise - Amen. He will always be remembered with love by his friends.

Away from the disciplined atmosphere of the Air Force, we tried to get the most enjoyment out of working in a civil outfit. Badeen Air Base, about two hour's drive from Hyderabad, became our parent unit for administration purposes. After reporting at CATI, we went to Badeen for the first report. On return, we created an imaginary, fictional secret order document kept at Badeen. Every Friday, the document needed the signatures of two course-attending officers. With Saturday and Sunday as a weekend, two officers would book out on Thursday after class in the pretense of signing the secret order in Badeen. We took turns enjoying the long weekends. As such, everyone enjoyed a long break once a month.

Air Traffic controlling in the Air Force, though following the basic operating rules of civil controlling, was a different ball game during the peak fighter flying hours. I remember during one of the annual Jet Stream exercises of the Air Force thirty-nine fighter jets of various types inflicted staggered attacks on the Masroor airfield from all directions in one-minute intervals. Only one controller provided service from the Control Tower without any radar service and only a mike in his hands. He would handle the entire attack by keeping a mental picture of all the attacking aircraft. He provided the needed separation and efficiently passed the information to the concerned air traffic.

Because of such demanding operations, it was not possible to follow the standards of separation directed by the manuals of International Civil Aviation Organization (ICAO). Air Force ATCOs gained greater confidence in handling the bulk of Air Traffic and in appreciation were called 'hot' controllers. Air Force ATCOs considered the Civil Controllers as 'D-Jays' (Disk Jockeys) performing in a dance party of fancy aircraft. Our opinion wasn't true, as we later realized. In fact, the civil safety measures were taken in respect for human life. However, with such a mindset, we landed at the CATI.

The first women Air Traffic Controllers of the Civil Aviation also attended the ATC course in separate classes at the same time. Another Air Traffic Controllers training course comprised of civilian controllers started at the same time.

Mr. Hanfi was the Director of the facility. He was a tall, smart, dark-coloured man with the serious look of an administrator. Mr. Zafar Sahi, the Dean of the Air Traffic Control facility, came from Lahore and spoke with a thick Lahori accent. He was a thorough professional, and had a friendly personality. All the other instructors were good ATC professionals and friendly in nature.

Unlike the other two civilian groups attending the ATC course, we had practical experience of all the material studied during the course. The course wasn't of much practical importance in the surroundings of Air Force controlling, but it fulfilled a valuable need in earning the civil controller's license. The license made a controller eligible to perform ATC duties anywhere in the world.

We decided to behave like carefree civilian teenage youngsters and called one another service names in keeping alive the motto of fun times during the course. Flight Lieutenant Moazzam was called Khan Sahab. His wise approach to in-service matters guided us through the problems. Flight Lieutenant Jan Nisar was nicknamed Johny. He took over running the officers' mess from the civil administration. Flight Lieutenant Asif was called Chum-Chum for his likeness to an advertising character and Flight Lieutenant Nabeel, named Billi for his innocent looks, helped Johny in performing the mess duties. They conducted the mess affairs by Air Force mess experience and provided tasty food for all its members. CATI administration was jubilant of this contribution by the Air Force Officers.

Flight Lieutenant Naseem Rizvi earned the title of hero for playing the flute. He played the flute every evening from the rooftop and mesmerized the entire mess atmosphere. Flight Lieutenant Shaukat Rasheed was called Shoka. Shoka generously shared his herbal medicine, falsely claiming it provided strength to various vital body parts. Flight Lieutenant Masood was termed Peter for his colourful dressing. Flight Lieutenant Sajid Mumtaz was called Bubbly for no obvious reason. I earned many titles to my account, but 'Ganja' was the most popular in representation of my bald head. Ten ATC officers of the Air Force, inspired by the public environment, went back in time to their student days of college. We formed an excellent, friendly bond with all the other civilian staff of CATI.

The PAF officers and the civil aviation members played a cricket match. I led the PAF cricket team, and Mr. Hanfi captained the CATI side. Mr. Hanfi, while batting, received a bad strike of the ball. Unfortunately, he hadn't been wearing the protective almond guard. We rushed him to the hospital. He stayed there for a few days during which time all the PAF officers regularly visited him and displayed genuine concern for his wellbeing.

Our course remained the favourite of Mr. Zafar Sahi, the Dean. One day when we were not happy with Mr. Sahi over some privilege issue, we planned on giving him a hard time. During his meteorology lecture he had taught something about an imaginative goat standing on the North Pole. If fired at, then she would escape the bullet because of the rotating Earth. In his theory, he tried his best to get the goat out of the way of the bullet. But with ten of us in a naughty mood, we brought the goat in the line of fire with our silly arguments every time. Mr. Sahi was at first confused but finally got the joke. He suspended the lecture, sat down on his desk, gave a big smile, and agreed to our earlier refused demand. We instantaneously accepted the concept that the goat had escaped the bullet.

Our rooms in the mess were full of bursting activities. Playing chess was a favourite pastime in my room. Supporters surrounded the two players and shouted like teenage schoolchildren. Shoka, Peter, and Khan Saab played chess in the master style.

Time passed quickly and our hour of departure arrived. Our mess team of Johny, Billi, and Chum had saved a handsome amount of money by producing even better food within the same allotted budget. CATI wasn't yet aware of the savings - we had planned to return the saved money at the end of the course.

The reason behind the success of mess affairs was the shopping by Billi from the local market. Instead of buying vegetables and meat from a contractor, he visited the public market once a week in Hyderabad and bought wholesale direct from the source. That effort resulted in fresh and cheap groceries.

A few days before our graduation we approached Mr. Hanfi, the Director and disclosed to him the saved amount. We asked permission to organize a music concert and a farewell party with the saved money. He was pleased and granted permission. We went out in the city and found a band of well-trained and educated singers - one of them was a dentist. They conducted a show that was attended by every CATI member in a grand style.

All of us graduated with flying colours. Like all good experiences, those few months of fun evaporated in the dust of time. Posting signals arrived at the Badeen Air Base sending ten of us to ten different bases of the Air Force. Mr. Hanfi and the civilian staff of CATI would never know about the clandestine fun behind the secret orders. Those were the days. Remembering them still brings joy to my heart.

*ATC Course at CATAI Hyderabad*
*PAF Air Traffic Control Officers standing behind*
*their ATC Instructors of the Civil Aviation*

*Moazzam, Farooq and Nusrat*

# Chapter Six
## The Jingle of Coins

In 1984, I served as an Air Traffic Control Officer (ATCO) at Chaklala Air Base, about twenty kilometres from the capital city of Islamabad. This was a joint user multi-purpose airfield used by the Air Force and the Civil Air Traffic. 'Chaklala Tower' and 'Islamabad International' were the two names of the same tower controlling arriving and departing traffic from the same runway. Air Commodore Mir Alam commanded the base and Group Captain Max served as Officer Commanding (OC) of the flying wing. Squadron Leader Salim Shahid was the Senior Air Traffic Control Officer (SATCO).

Besides the Air Force ATCOs there were four Controllers provided by the department of Civil Aviation. Sparing an ATC officer for leave in the Air Force remained a challenge because of the shortage of Controllers. However, because of the presence of four Civil Aviation Controllers, sparing an ATCO for leave abroad was not a big issue in the ATC Squadron of Chaklala. Every PAF officer was entitled to thirty days annual leave within Pakistan and forty-five days Ex-Pakistan leave abroad. Yet some Air Force commanders did not like sending their officers on leave even when the conditions were favourable.

I had applied for a forty-five day leave abroad to England and France. My immediate boss, the SATCO, recommended my leave abroad application to OC Flying Wing. My leave application was to be recommended by OC and Base Commander before final approval of the Air Headquarters (A.H.Q.). The A.H.Q. finally approved the leave after gathering the intelligence clearance about the officer. This was the typical procedure that was followed for the approval of Ex-Pakistan leave of an officer of the Air Force.

I could sense a threat to my leave-taking when Squadron Leader Shahid, SATCO told me that OC Flying had asked me to report to his office. I had a fair idea about what was in store for me at the office of OC Flying. I prepared myself by reading the Air Force manual regarding leave and reported to his office.

After I entered his office and saluted, OC used the usual phrase to deny the leave: "You know that we are short of officers and sparing you for leave will not be easy."

"Sir, the SATCO has spared me because we also have four Civil Air Traffic Controllers to man the Control Tower," I humbly replied.

"You have been on leave abroad in the previous year also?" the OC shifted position.

"Yes Sir. I have read the Air Force law about Ex-Pakistan leave-taking," I softly cautioned him. It was not a demerit. The Air Force rule about Ex-Pakistan leave stated that an officer of the Air Force could go on leave abroad for two successive years, after which a gap of two years was compulsory.

Not impressed by my knowledge of the Air Force law, the OC tried to advance in a different direction,

"Why do you want to go again?"

I honestly replied,

"Because, Sir, my brothers living abroad are paying the expense for the visit and it is a golden chance to spend some time with family."

Group Captain Max with a wise look on his face inquired,

"What is the fault of the other officers whose brothers cannot afford to pay the expenses for their visit abroad?"

I could hardly believe my ears. I stood startled with my mouth hanging open in disbelief at his argument. I responded, now almost crying,

"Is it a fault Sir that my brothers can afford to pay the expenses for my visit?"

I knew that my argument had puzzled him. He thought for a second and spoke with authority, "Flight Lieutenant Nusrat, I know your visit has been arranged by your brothers so I will let you go, but I am using my discretional powers to cut short your leave to twenty-one days. I am not denying your leave." He warned me by looking straight into my eyes.

Denial of leave could have provided me with a convincing opportunity to approach the Base Commander, but cutting short the leave reduced my chances of success with the higher ranks. I stood silent in deep thought with my brain quickly estimating my travelling time and the time I intended to spend with my brothers.

Finding me quiet and speechless, OC announced his victory with a smile on his face, "Flight Lieutenant Nusrat, you think you are too damn smart... well you are not."

My intelligence had been challenged. I didn't like to see myself as less intelligent than the OC. I gathered up all my senses, looked back with a wicked smile on my face, and said, apparently surrendering,

"Yes Sir, thank you very much. I will go for only twenty-one days."

Now it was the OC's turn to be mute and serious. He had been sure that I would not accept such a short leave period for such a long journey. My response probably astonished him, and so he spoke again with a commanding voice in order to confirm his victory,

"In that case you will file a new application asking leave for twenty-one days only."

"Yes Sir, I will file a new application for twenty-one days only." He did not want to leave the pen scar of cruelty on the application, but I knew when to use that to my advantage. I saluted with full force before leaving his office.

Both of us had smiles on our faces. He carried the smile of a victor. I carried different meanings in my wicked smile to be unfolded later.

A fresh application for twenty-one days abroad was filed, freshly recommended by the SATCO. The application went through the proper channels and finally I was cleared to go abroad on a twenty-one day leave. I went to London first to stay with my sister Shahnaz. Later, as arranged by my brothers Ishrat and Kuckoo, I joined them in Paris.

Time passed quickly in Paris. Soon, I realized that if I did not board a plane back home for Pakistan, I would be absent without official leave (AWOL) from my place of duty.

It was noontime in Paris which, according to the time zone difference, meant five o'clock in the evening in Pakistan. The Base Commander, Air Commodore Mir Alam, according to his routine, should be at his home at this hour of the day.

Being an Air Traffic Control Officer I remained in direct contact with the Base Commander. My job often demanded contacting him on the hotline by telephone or walkie-talkie depending on his available position. I knew about the bold and friendly nature of Air Commodore Mir Alam. In my mind I was confident that I had a special rapport with the commander. The moment for testing my confidence had arrived.

I quietly came out with my brothers Ishrat and Kuckoo from the Villa at Merri the Lilla and walked a few hundred feet down the street to the telephone booth. French francs jingled in my pocket as I entered the telephone booth and dialed the official number of the Base Commander's residence in Pakistan.

As expected, Air Commodore Mir Alam, the Base Commander picked up the telephone.

"Mir Alam," I heard the familiar voice.

"Good evening, Sir, or rather it is good afternoon here. I am Flight Lieutenant Nusrat calling from Paris."

"Hello, Nusrat, how are you doing in Paris?"

"Sir, I am fine, and as you know I had applied for a leave of twenty-one days only."

I reminded the Base Commander of my intent to go abroad for twenty-one days only. It was rare that anyone applied for only twenty-one days leave abroad. The time had come for the use of OC's tactics to my advantage.

"Yes, I wondered," he replied.

"Sir, because of reasons unexplainable on the telephone, I need my leave to be extended for another fifteen days," I requested.

"Do you mean that you want fifteen more days?" The Base Commander asked.

"Yes Sir," I briefly replied.

There was a short pause and then from a distance came the voice of the Base Commander.

"No problem, Nusrat, you can have fifteen more days and come back safely," he replied graciously.

"Thank you very much, Sir," I replied in haste, and despite a strong desire to shout 'Long Live Sir Mir Alam', I calmly disconnected the line.

My next call was to SATCO Shahid. I informed him about the extension in leave by the Base Commander. He laughed when I asked him to convey this to the OC Flying.

In my imagination I remembered the OC, and his words echoed in my mind one more time: "Flight Lieutenant Nusrat, you think you are too damn smart... well you are not."

The French coins jingled in my pocket as I walked back through the streets of Paris. It seemed that this is when my vacation really started.

If you are thinking this is the climax and the end of the story, well, you are wrong. It would end on a double climax. My coursemate Squadron Leader Azhar Syed, who was then serving the ISI, had recommended my name as his replacement to the ISI. Commodore S.M.K. Zaidi in the Inter-Services Intelligence (ISI) interviewed me. Air Force did not have any knowledge about this interview. I had told Commodore Zaidi about my intent of going on leave abroad. We had agreed I would join the ISI on return from leave.

I was also in touch from abroad with Squadron Leader Azhar Rana who was in the Air Secretary Branch of Air Headquarters responsible for initiating the posting signals. After the extension in leave, I requested Squadron Leader Rana from Paris to mention delaying the reporting date at ISI by a few days after my return to Pakistan. Azhar Rana is a genuinely noble soul of the Air Force. He graciously accepted the request and therefore the signal of my posting was issued.

At the expiry of my extended leave, I reported to ATC Squadron Chaklala. I was promoted to the rank of a Squadron Leader and my posting out signal from Chaklala was issued on my return from leave. A day before going out from Chaklala to the ISI, the OC ordered SATCO Shahid not to release me from the ATC Squadron. He wasn't prepared to let me go so easily. He wanted to have another round of this ping-pong game.

I was worried and sensed cancellation of my posting. From the Control Tower of Chaklala, I called the ISI Head Quarters and informed them what I had been told by Squadron Leader Shahid. The furious voice of the ISI Commander asked,

"Who has told you to stay back?"

This was the kind of voice I wished to hear. Officers serving with the ISI always considered themselves above other military officers. Very politely submitting to his furious voice, I replied, "Sir, I have been told by my SATCO, Squadron Leader Shahid, that the OC Flying has held me back. However, I have not been given any reason and the SATCO doesn't have any problem in sparing me, Sir."

Before hanging up the phone he responded angrily, "We will see!"

About fifteen minutes later the hotline with SATCO buzzed in the Control Tower. When I picked up the receiver, I heard the bursting laughter of Squadron Leader Shaid. He asked,

"What have you done?"

Worried and clueless, I replied, "What, Sir?"

He said, "The OC called me just now and said, tell him immediately to f---k off from here."

That is the best use of this four-letter word I have ever enjoyed hearing in my honour. I ran down the Control Tower stairs, the Pakistani coins in my pocket jingling with joy.

# Chapter Seven
## Once a Comrade, Always a Comrade

### Switching to Cockpit in the Air

In 1982, I was promoted to Flight Lieutenant and posted back to PAF Base Masroor in Karachi. The Rescue Squadron, which was next door to the Control Tower, consisted of H-43 helicopters. These Korean War model choppers were old and haggard, but they carried hearts as young as their carefree pilots. The ATC Officers and Rescue Squadron pilots enjoyed healthy relations because of their near ground position and similar shift duties.

We remained in position at our respective places of responsibility when jet flying was in progress. But during the afternoon shifts or the lull hours, we visited each other's locations for friendly chats and to play board games of scrabble and chess. Those were the essential sports items available in all the flying crew rooms and the Control Towers of the Air Force. We enjoyed each other's hospitality over samosas, sandwiches, or the famous shami kebabs of the officers' mess of Masroor.

I enjoyed good relations with most of the helicopter pilots. Flight Lieutenants Pervez Samuel and Naveed Sabahat were my seniors from Risalpur Academy days and Flight Lieutenant Maula was my coursemate serving in Rescue Squadron at the time. Flying Officer Shahid Tufail of the Rescue Squadron, a young junior officer, became a close friend because of our similar views and compatibility with the board games. My closeness to Flying Officer Shahid upgraded my condition with the Rescue Squadron to 'chum status' and I was put on the frequent flyer list.

One day, not knowing what lay ahead, I boarded one of the routine fun flights for buzzing over the Hawks Bay beach. Flying Officer Shahid occupied the copilot's seat in the cockpit, and Sir Sheharyar - Shery, as we called him - was the Captain-in-Command. Flying Officer Shahid suddenly unstrapped himself from the cockpit and joined me in the back cabin, where I sat casually looking over the sea. Well, what dumbfounded me was the route he took. He had come from outside the helicopter as if he was on a stroll in a park while flying about one thousand feet above the sea. Had I not known him and his respectable family, I would have been convinced that he had a previous career in the railways working in the dining car. His calm demeanour needed just that background of moving trays from one bogey to another so fearlessly in a moving train. What he told me next sapped the energy from my legs. He looked at me with a naughty smile and said,

"Sir, the captain wants you to take the copilot seat."

The testing moment had arrived; Shahid wasn't joking. He wanted to check out my guts. I had to go the same way from outside the helicopter, flying about one thousand feet above the sea. I wasn't interested in controlling the chopper at the cost of my life, but the thought of living with the stigma of 'coward' for the rest of my life was even worse. Images of my wife and daughter Maheen who was couple of years young at the time came to my mind; what would they make of my adventure if it turned into an untimely free fall?

The next image of a big chicken chasing me was not worth living. I silently got up, took a deep breath, looked down once, held the metal bar of the cabin with one hand, and almost jumped into the vacant copilot seat by holding the edge of the cockpit with my other hand. In fact, a little emergency was created as I unintentionally pressed the collective pitch lever. The helicopter sank fast momentarily, but Sir Shery was used to such panic entries and had been expecting it. He immediately controlled the helicopter as I sank in the copilot seat.

I enjoyed flying the remaining mission. However, I had to make this move one more time as the Standing Operating Procedure (SOP) demanded to land back with the same cockpit crew that had taken off from the base. Helicopter pilots were serious about following the SOPs! This time, it was rather easy. My mind filled with the joy of a brave chopper flying experience; maybe, in my previous life, I might have served in the railways as well.

# On the Taxi Track

Air Force personnel and their families enjoyed the privilege of free rides on the Hercules C-130 aircraft. Though they mainly delivered equipment and other necessary goods from one Air Force base to another, there was always enough space to carry passengers in its huge belly.

Travelling by C-130 was no less than an adventure. Travellers, including the women and children, sat on the folding red canvas seats attached to light silver metallic bars. Instead of the beautiful air hostesses in a commercial airliner, one noted the stout load-masters efficiently taking care of the technical issues inside the flying aircraft. Toilets were not available. This small inconvenience helped save money. Commercial airfare for four family members was more than the monthly salary of a junior officer. The Pakistan Air Force C-130 flights did not follow a strict regular schedule like a commercial airline. They operated on an as-needed basis by the Air Force - though Air Force personnel posted far away from their native homes often planned their holidays with free C-130 rides. Free rides were graciously available for all men and officers of the Air Force.

Once, after spending holidays in Islamabad with my parents, I booked the free ride with my wife and daughter Maheen to return to my place of duty in Karachi. On the day of departure, we reported late to the Air Movement office responsible for issuing boarding passes and handling of luggage. When I reached the counter, I saw from a lounge window that the aircraft had started its four turboprop engines and was about to roll out of the parking bay. I knew that Flight Lieutenant Kazim Ali Awan, my course-mate, was the captain; he was also aware of my seat in his aircraft. I grabbed the boarding passes, asked my wife to follow, and ran out of the Air Movement building. The majestic C-130 by then had started taxiing. I waved with one hand to stop the aircraft as if signalling for a cab to stop. I rolled my suitcase with the other hand. Kazim, on seeing me from the cockpit and my wife running behind holding our two-year-old daughter Maheen, stopped the aircraft. The cockpit door opened and the ladder lowered. We hurriedly climbed in. As I looked at the smiling face of Kazim, I winked back at him, and stepped into the cabin towards our seats in the plane.

We did not create any flight safety hazard. However, we were sure to get letters of displeasure had someone from the higher authorities seen our unusual boarding. These were the risks we happily took to serve our comrades in arms. Kazim retired as an Air Commodore after commanding the Chaklala Air Base.

# Engine Malfunction

Air Base Shore Kot in the Jhang District, about three hundred fifty kilometres from Islamabad, was renamed Rafiqui Air Base to honour Squadron Leader Sarfraz Ahmed Rafiqui. He was a decorated fighter pilot who received Hilal-e-Jurat - the second highest gallantry award and Sitara-e-Jurat - the third highest gallantry military award of Pakistan. He fought bravely during the 1965 India-Pakistan War. In the end, jammed guns during a midair battle brought him down. He embraced martyrdom around Halwara Air Base in India.

In the year 1985, I was posted at the Rafiqui Air Base. One day I received the flight plan of a C-130 inbound from Karachi heading to Islamabad. The aircraft carried Base Commanders from all of the Air Bases to attend a monthly Flight Safety meeting at the Air Headquarters in Chaklala. Squadron Leader Qamar Zaman Bhatti, the senior air traffic control officer (SATCO) and my boss, approved my leave to take advantage of a free ride on the C-130 aircraft. I called my wife by phone and asked her to get ready soon. She was used to our scrambled departures.

When Flight Lieutenant Mushtaq Chaudhry, my coursemate and captain of the aircraft, contacted the tower by radio, the plane was a few hundred miles away from Shore Kot. I asked him to wait for me as I had to pick up my wife and children from home. Knowing well the local transport conditions, the VIP flight status of his aircraft, and my lack of efficiency, he warned me to be on time. He had to pick up the Rafiqui Base Commander with running engines without wasting any time.

Rafiqui Air Base had two officers' living quarter areas. The colony area where I lived was at a driving distance of fifteen to twenty minutes from the Control Tower, where I was on duty. A track of the Pakistan Railways ran between the road joining the Technical area and the living quarters of the Base. In the case of a closed gate at the railway crossing, one had to wait for ten to fifteen extra minutes.

I got on the Motorola radio-fitted ATC jeep after having received communication with the tower. After picking up my family from the officers' mess, I rushed back to catch the plane. So far, I was within my time constraints - until I reached the railway track crossing to find the gate locked. The locked gate meant a minimum of ten minutes delay on my estimated time of arrival. On the other hand, Mushtaq had no valid reason to hold after Base Commander Rafiqui boarded the plane with engines running. My ground position, when relayed to Mushtaq by the tower, left him with no choice. He switched off the two left engines, pretending technical issue of the aircraft. When after ten minutes I approached the C-130 on the tarmac, I saw the two left engines switched off. A Flight Engineer was working on one engine while the other two engines on the right were kept running. Mushtaq signaled me through the windscreen of the cockpit to board from the rear ramp as the aircraft carried the VIPs. As soon as I stepped on the rear ramp, the unserviceable engines suddenly came back to life, and soon we were airborne. Several one-star Generals on board the aircraft never knew the real reason for the delay on the ground.

Mushtaq took early retirement from the PAF as a Squadron Leader and is now working as a Boeing 737NG Captain with one of the national airlines.

*Sqn. Ldr. Mushtaq Ahmad Chaudhry*

*Air Commodore Kazim*

*Wing Cdr. Shaharyar*

*Shahid and Minhas*

*From left Adnan, Ma Ji, Mohib, Mohammed, Shaheen and Nusrat. Imran standing behind and Maheen sitting in front.*

# Chapter Eight
## Dangling in the Air

## To All Fighter Pilots of the World

Speed thrills, but kills. Hasty actions are required if you like to enjoy the thrill of speed. During fighter flying, swift actions sometimes become the only difference between life and death. The following two chapters "Dangling in the Air" and "Flights to Heaven" are chapters of action and inaction. I realized while writing and discussing the stories of these pilots that their timely action or inaction to eject ultimately contributed to either saving or terminating their lives.

Another interesting factor of following good habitual practice came to my attention while writing about the ejection story of AVM Abbas Mirza. He told me that he had adopted a habit of always practicing a dry face blind ejection procedure after getting in the cockpit. Every time he got in the cockpit of his fighter aircraft, he performed a dry ejection procedure by swiftly moving his hands over all the required handles and adopting the ejection posture stipulated in the checklist. In my opinion, his well-ingrained habit largely contributed to saving his life when he ejected out of the F-6 cockpit from 600 feet above ground.

The mirage crash landing story of Flight Lieutenant Masood Karim reveals what he remembered from his academy days of taking his feet away from the rudders while crash landing in an uneven field. The stories of Flight Lieutenant Rizvi and Flight Lieutenant S.T. Chaudhry reveal the inaction that resulted in taking their lives. After going through all these recollections, I realized that the lessons contained in these stories are very important for the knowledge of every fighter pilot in any Air Force of the world. Therefore, I strongly recommend that you - all fighter pilots of the world - read these stories and extract lessons of your own. May the Almighty God save your wings and keep you safely soaring in the air. Good luck and happy landings.

# Duzz, Duzz, Duzz - Blasts in the Air!

### FIRST F-6 MARTIN-BAKER SEAT (MK-10D) EJECTION

Wing Commander Zahid Malik was an instructor pilot of T-37 aircraft during my cadetship from 1976-1978 at the Risalpur Academy of the Pakistan Air Force. We met again in 2014 in Vancouver, Canada. While discussing my book with him, he mentioned that, coincidentally, he was the first pilot of the Pakistan Air Force who ejected using the famous **Martin-Baker (Mk-10D)** ejection seat from F-6 aircraft. The incident happened on the 21st of March, 1975, a few months before my joining the Air Force, and I was so interested that I asked for details of the episode. Wing Commander Zahid recounted the incident with the sequence of events that helped put this piece together. The following lines carry the episode of the first Martin-Baker seat ejection from F-6 aircraft by Flying Officer Malik.

Flying Officer Malik, on his first posting as an operational pilot, flew for No.15 Squadron of F-6 (Mig-19) aircraft at Air Base Peshawar. A technical problem of the bleed bands not opening often occurred in the F-6 aircraft. The increased compressor stalls of the aircraft at circuit altitude caused fatal crashes. Bleed bands are metallic bands around each engine compressor which discharge extra air through small rectangular windows (four on each side behind the canopy) at the mid-section of the fuselage. These bands bleed extra air generated by compressors at below 9,500 rpm of engines. As the rpm of both engines goes above 9,500, the bleed bands should close to give maximum thrust to engines for takeoff at maximum rpm 11,200 of F-6 aircraft. Similarly, as the throttles are brought back, the bleed bands should open; otherwise the engine would stall (compressor stall). This rarely happened, but the not closing or not opening of bleed bands at the required rpm could cause a serious emergency.

Ejection attempts made through the original Chinese-fitted ejection seats had failed miserably, and loss of pilots became a concern for the Air Force. Thus, Air Headquarters (AHQ) contacted the Martin-Baker Company, British manufacturer of the ejection seats.

The company, originally founded by Sir James Martin as the Martin Aircraft Manufacturer, became the Martin-Baker Aircraft Company when it was joined by Captain Valentine Baker in 1938. Captain Baker died in an air crash in 1942. Grieved by his death, Sir Martin began focusing on pilot safety. His company designed a forced ejection system with the pilot sitting in the seat. After conducting different altitude and speed limit tests on ejection seats, Martin-Baker introduced the zero-zero capability seat which confirmed a safe ejection at zero speed and zero altitude. This meant that a pilot, while sitting in the cockpit of a parked aircraft, could execute a safe ejection even from the ground.

When the Air Headquarters contacted Martin-Baker, they designed and installed a zero-zero ability ejection seat in the cockpit of an F-6 aircraft of No.15 Squadron. It was a relaxing seat with comfortable straps. In addition, a weight machine was placed in the squadron. Every pilot flying the only F-6 aircraft fitted with the Martin-Baker (MB) seat was weighed before getting into the cockpit. The seat needed the exact weight setting for correct trajectory in case of ejection. Squadron pilots always desired to fly this aircraft that had been fitted with the MB seat. On the 21st of March, 1975 Flying Officer Zahid was scheduled to fly a Dissimilar Air Combat Training (DACT) mission against a pair of F-86 aircraft flown by his previous instructor pilots of No. 26 Squadron. He was glad that the MB seat fitted F-6 aircraft had been assigned to him. Zahid got airborne in the supersonic cockpit of the F-6 for a dogfight against the subsonic F-86's flown by his experienced instructors. The idiom 'No shortcut to experience' prevailed. Young Zahid was thrown off in combat by the experienced pilots of the subsonic F-86 aircraft. He flicked at 12,000 feet and entered into a spin.

Standard Operating Procedure (SOP) demanded ejection if one did not recover out of a spin by 10,000 feet. His confidence from sitting in the high performance MB ejection seat encouraged Zahid to continue with the recovery procedure even after crossing 10,000 feet. He continued his effort to recover until crossing 7000 feet. At that point he realized that any further delay in ejection could take him into a big black hole in the ground to burn with the aircraft. His hand reached the panhandle and he pulled it. Duzz, duzz, and duzz sounded three blasts, and he found himself hanging with the chute blossomed above his head. He was dangling in absolute quietness and serene air. The world below promised him a second life. He looked down and saw the ground fast approaching his feet. Suddenly he found himself sitting on the backpack which he had failed to separate manually. He had heard that ejection always induced some bruises on the body, if not a broken bone. Finding himself clean without any pain surprised him. He took a few jumps to ensure that his body worked fine. Mixed feelings of joy and surprise surfaced in his mind as he gathered his parachute and waited for the rescue chopper to pick him up. The aircraft burned a few feet away, randomly firing the blast bullets from the wreckage.

The ejection was perfect, despite taking latitude with the delay in getting out. His timely action kept him alive. The story does not end here, for another surprise awaited him. He had ejected in the tribal area of Pakistan governed by Pathans under tribal law. He saw some Pathans from a nearby market (Bara market) rushing towards him with guns pointed in his direction. What would happen if some trigger-happy Pathan decided to test his gun? They considered him an enemy pilot who had illegally landed on their territory.

Finding himself 'out of the frying pan and into the fire', he silently stood there like a deer being encircled by a gradually approaching squad of hunters. An uneasy silence prevailed as he didn't know their language. Suddenly, a young boy approached him from behind and said,

"Sir, I am an airman working in the Air Traffic Control of Peshawar Base."

Without wasting a moment, Zahid pulled the boy from behind and held him in front. He whispered into the ear of the airman to ask them to put down their guns. The hostile Pathans withdrew their guns after hearing the airman speaking in their Pushto language.

A big crowd gathered around Zahid to take a good peek at the surviving pilot. They took him to the office of the 'Tehsildar' (Deputy Commissioner), leaving behind a person to tell the rescue helicopter about his position in the office. Hearing the sound of the landing chopper, Zahid headed out of the office only to see the helicopter heading back to the base without him. Someone from the crowd had told the chopper pilot that he had gone by road to the Base. He then asked the Tehsildar to arrange for his travel back to the Base. The distance was not too far - about ten kilometres by road. They finally arranged a rickety Wagoner that brought him back to the base. Despite all the hardships, he was happy to be alive and safe. An air of joy and festivity prevailed at the base – not only because Zahid was alive, but also because the new ejection seat of Martin-Baker had passed the test on F-6 aircraft. Everyone wanted to know about the ejection seat. The Air Chief was also pleased with the successful ejection from the

Martin-Baker seat. The Accident Investigating Officer of the Flight Safety Directorate asked Zahid,

"Why did you enter into a spin?"

The question was so abrupt that a fighter pilot would have to think carefully before answering it. Zahid was at loss for words to respond to the question - and he is still today, even after forty-odd years. Wing Commander Zahid retired after commanding the No. 5 squadron of mirage aircraft of the Pakistan Air Force. He now teaches aviation at a university in Dubai.

# Aircraft Just Landed; You are on Fire – Eject!

Air Commodore Amjad Bashir was my roommate for more than two years in Lower Topa and Risalpur during our cadetship days. We cherish many fond memories of the Risalpur Academy. We shared bunk beds. I occupied the upper bunk while Amjad took the lower bunk. Ibrahim, our dedicated and loyal batman, served us in his unique style with his innocent follies providing lots of entertainment for the entire course.

We started each day by rising together for the early morning run (popularly known as the morning jerks), then rushed to the dining hall for meals. We attended the same classes in the Education Directorate. Together we marched in the parade ground, and we went to the same squadron for flying. We shared the punishment given by seniors during the day. At night we returned to our bunk beds.

Coursemates named our room the Nikko, Nakka room - Nikko for his short height and Nakka for my big nose. Even a husband and a wife do not live in such togetherness after the honeymoon. Well, the cadets living in the academy had a honeymoon period that lasted for more than a couple of years. In our case we not only shared but enjoyed every moment of our blessed company. Comradeship is built in a similar manner - being prepared to live and die together. Amjad candidly narrated to me his experience after ejecting from an F-6 aircraft.

Amjad, then a Flight Lieutenant, moved from Sargodha to Kamra Air Base with his squadron because of the carpeting of the Sargodha runway. He then belonged to No. 25 squadron of F-6 aircraft that trained the pilots to gain operational status after graduating from the fighter conversion unit. He acted as an Instructor Pilot of No. 25 squadron.

On the sunny morning of June 21st, 1982, Amjad got airborne on a chase mission with his student, Pilot Officer Tanveer, nicknamed 'Tarzan' because of his thin physique. In a chase mission the student technically maintains a call sign of No. 2, but remains ahead throughout the formation and is observed by the Leader chasing from behind or formatting as wingman. The leader observes and guides the student on various preplanned exercises. While coming back for landing, the student remains in front and the leader positions him as a wingman separated by 300 feet according to the standard operating procedure for chase position. This position is maintained from initials reporting point to pitchout, base turn, and on finals from where the student lands full stop on the runway while the leader executes a go round to land in a subsequent approach. The instructor or leader, besides his own protection, carries the larger responsibility of the safe return of his No. 2, the student pilot. The formation returned to the circuit after familiarization of the flying area. A circuit is a standard flying path a few miles around the airfield. Aircraft while landing follow this path by maintaining visual contact with the runway.

On the first low-go approach, Amjad twice asked his student to check that the landing gears were down at the base turn. During a low-go approach a pilot follows the standard landing pattern in the circuit, but instead of landing on the runway, he goes around from the final stage of landing. Base leg is a position from where an aircraft initiates its turn to align with the runway on the final approach.

Amjad's student confirmed the three green lights and the three protruding mechanical indicators. Satisfied with the approach of his number two, they initiated the low-go with the leader chasing behind.

They again entered the landing pattern, this time for a full stop landing by the student pilot. On the base turn, Amjad again asked the student to check the three green lights confirming the down position of the landing gear. The student, helped by the instructor, again positioned himself nicely on the final approach.

On the short final position before landing, Amjad reported low-go for himself and handed over the student to Mobile for a full stop landing. Flight Lieutenant Maratib was the other instructor pilot performing the duty of the Mobile officer. Mobile is a small hut built at the landing threshold of the runway as a mini control tower. It is manned by an operational pilot of the type of the aircraft offering help in an emergency. However, the main role of the Mobile officer is to visually check that the landing gears are in the down position for all the aircraft on final approach. Mobile ensured that Pilot Officer Tanveer, student of Amjad, landed safely.

Amjad asked the Air Traffic Control Tower to pull a 'Close' - a short circuit pattern joining maneuvre that directly placed the aircraft on the inner downwind position before base leg. Pilot Officer Haider from the Control Tower directed Amjad to delay his pull up as two other aircraft were reporting at the 'Initials' position in the circuit pattern. Position 'Initials' is at fifteen hundred feet above ground and a couple of miles abeam one end of the landing runway.

Amjad delayed his pull up and spaced himself well as number three behind the two aircraft inbound from Initials position in the landing pattern. When he reached a position opposite to the Control Tower, Flight Lieutenant Kamran, in a dual cockpit FT-6 with his student, asked for clearance from the tower for a straight-in approach. A straight-in approach comes within 30 degrees of the landing runway without making a turn. As there were already three aircraft in the landing pattern, Pilot Officer Haider from the Control Tower asked him to make an orbit at the long final position about 15 miles away in line with the landing runway. Amjad, after adjusting No. 3 in the landing pattern, reduced to landing speed and lowered the landing gear lever in the cockpit. He did not look at the three greens as the aircraft in front of him made a loose base turn and he adjusted behind by keeping the other aircraft in sight. Flight Lieutenant Kamran, after completing the orbit on the long final position, reported short on fuel and was thus considered priority landing. ATC cleared him for final approach behind Amjad who also had to make a wider base turn. A worried Amjad tried to find Flight Lieutenant Kamran by turning right on the final approach, but he could not see him.

At the same moment the drag-chute of the aircraft ahead of Amjad snapped after landing on the runway. A drag-chute is a parachute designed to be deployed by a fighter jet aircraft to slow down and shorten the landing run. Mobile and the ATC simultaneously transmitted a snap shoot call that created some rush on the radio. Amjad meanwhile reached the short finals when he heard the frantic repeated calls from the mobile: "Aircraft on short finals go round." The Mobile Officer did not use the call sign of the aircraft ordered to go round. Amjad assumed that Flight Lieutenant Kamran had closed in behind him and was being asked to go round. He asked which aircraft to go round, and expected to see Flight Lieutenant Kamran going round above him as there was no other aircraft in the landing sequence.

Mobile continued shouting the go round calls without using the call sign of any aircraft. By that time Amjad had crossed the threshold of the runway, so he rotated the nose and flared out by bringing the throttle back to the idle position for touchdown. He felt that something was wrong as the wheels were not touching down. The aircraft sank and suddenly he heard the hard rubbing sound of metal with heavy juddering. All the instruments turned red in the cockpit and he could see dust flying around. As an instant reaction, he looked at the landing lever, and finding it in neutral position, he shouted "Shit!" He knew exactly what had happened - he had landed on the flat belly without the landing gear. At the same moment he heard repeated calls from the mobile, "Aircraft just landed, you are on fire - eject." He recited "Kalima" (religious verses) and pulled the ejection handle. Seconds later he found himself hanging in the air with a parachute while gradually falling down towards the ground. Amjad survived a zero level, zero speed ejection, thus becoming the 5,291st survivor of the Martin-Baker (MB seat PKD-10) according to their records. Martin-Baker keeps a record of all the survivors who have used their ejection seat. According to Amjad, this series of mishaps occurred because of Murphy's Law - everything that could go wrong, went wrong in a sequence. He twice checked the gears of his student on full stop landing, but forgot to lower his own gears. In the F-6 aircraft it is important to bring the landing lever to the neutral position after raising the landing gear. When he delayed his pull for close he forgot to bring down the landing lever to neutral from the up position as he was adjusting in the landing pattern behind the two other aircraft.

On the inner downwind position, when he lowered the landing lever down, he had in fact brought it to the neutral position - but his mind registered lowering of the landing gear. Emergency calls of snap shoot and low-on-fuel came within the span of one minute. The aircraft ahead of him made a wider base turn. He remained busily adjusting his position by looking outside the cockpit for other aircraft. It was too late when he finally looked at the landing lever.

Each of the three main characters engaged in this scenario missed some necessary action on their part:

Amjad missed the three greens call at the base leg while adjusting his position and blocked R/T by the tower and the mobile due to the snapped shoot.

ATC did not notice that the three greens call was missed at the base turn and issued the landing clearance.

When the mobile officer spotted the aircraft without gear down on short finals, he ordered the go round without using the call sign of the aircraft.

The Board of Inquiry blamed all three characters. Flight Lieutenant Amjad and Flight Lieutenant Maratib, the Mobile Officer, received six months of loss of seniority. Pilot Officer Haider, the officer in the Control Tower, was awarded three months loss of seniority. None of them felt badly about their respective punishments because Flight Lieutenant Amjad had survived the deadly crash. Amjad later retired from service after rising to the rank of Air Commodore.

# Tossed out of the Cockpit

Squadron Leader Imtiaz Ahmed was my senior from the 64th G.D.(P.) course. In 1978 we served together at the Air Force Base Masroor in Karachi. We enjoyed friendly relations from our academy days and often dined together at the officers' mess. Imtiaz at that time was posted to No. 17 Squadron while I served the Air Traffic Control Squadron. Two years later, I was posted out of Masroor to Cherat and Imtiaz was transferred to Fighter Instructor School at the Air Force Academy of Risalpur. At Risalpur, Imtiaz also flew with the prestigious 'Sher-Dil' formation assigned to perform aerobatics during the graduation ceremony of pilots. After completing his tenure as an instructor at the academy he was posted back to Masroor Air Base to No. 19 squadron of the F-6 aircraft.

Exercise 'flat-out' to test the maximum efficiency of the fighter squadrons was routinely conducted by the Air Force. Every squadron on the prescribed day of exercise would fly maximum sorties testing its pilots, aircraft, and the engineering staff. This exercise also kept the Air Traffic Controllers restricted within the glass house who otherwise enjoyed leisure time during lulls in flying.

On the beautiful afternoon of March 30th, 1985, while participating in exercise 'flat-out', Imtiaz took off for his fourth sortie of the day leading a two-ship formation. He occupied the front seat of a FT-6 dual pilot (DP) aircraft while Flying Officer Salman Aslam sat in the rear cockpit. Flying Officer Javed Ahmed followed as his wingman from the cockpit of another F-6 aircraft. The mission was planned for a medium level cine to be followed by tail chase on return to the base. During a medium level cine mission, the aircraft engage in a dogfight between 15,000 to 20,000 feet. After completing the cine mission, the leader asked his number two, Flying Officer Javed, to take over the lead and he adjusted behind in tail chase position. Imtiaz relaxed back in his seat, casually formatting behind his appointed leader. They were flying over the 'Uthal' hilly Baluchistan area when Imtiaz suddenly heard a big bang that threw him unconscious out of the cockpit of his aircraft.

Flying Officer Salman, sitting in the rear cockpit, suddenly saw a huge spark followed by a big bang that took Imtiaz flying out of the cockpit. His vision was momentarily blinded and he was frozen in shock. Unaware of what the hell had gone wrong, he quickly decided to follow his captain and pulled the ejection handle by transmitting "No. 2 ejecting." He was tossed out of the cockpit. His chute blossomed perfectly as he started his descent from about 16,000 feet and it took him about fifteen minutes to touch the ground.

During his parachute descent, Salman kept looking around in a joyless attempt to locate the parachute of Imtiaz who had left the cockpit before him. Salman remembers making a perfect parachute landing fall (PLF) learned at the PAF academy. Finding himself on a small hillock in the complete wilderness with no soul in sight, he spread out his brightly coloured parachute on ground for the convenience of the rescue helicopter. His wrist watch, which had stopped functioning, was stuck at 2:22 pm, thus indicating the exact time of ejection. He took out the flares from the rescue kit attached with the parachute and tried to think about what had happened.

After hearing the call of Salman, Flying Officer Javed turned around to see the falling parachute. He circled over the crash site and transmitted his position to the control tower about the ejection of the other aircraft. Radar controllers of the air defence marked his position, search and rescue action was immediately activated by the Masroor Control Tower, and two helicopters got airborne to recover their pilots.

Upon regaining consciousness about forty-five minutes later, Imtiaz found himself lying on the ground with soaring hills all around. Gradual recollection of events made him aware of the cause of his presence in that wilderness. He was bleeding and experiencing shooting pain in his head, back, and ankle. He had no clue about what had transpired. It was a smooth flight, he had never even touched the handle of the reliable Martin Baker ejection seat installed in his aircraft, but something extremely extraordinary had gone wrong. He could only remember a bang that tossed him out of the cockpit. There was no recollection of how the chute had blossomed or how he had landed on the ground. This present state of affairs made him aware of his severe body ache, his missing helmet, the extreme heat, and a parachute that trapped him.

He shouted for help many times at the top of his voice, but his words returned with an echo after striking the surrounding hills. After some time he heard a hammering sound that gradually turned into the noise of the helicopter rotors. This sound kindled a ray of hope, for he knew that the search and rescue helicopters had come to pick him up. Joy appeared on his face as he considered this to be the end of his ordeal. To attract the attention of the rescue copter he fired the flares out of the survival kit attached with the parachute, but the two helicopters hovered away from his position and soon left the site.

Helicopters soon spotted Salman who was sitting beside his perfectly laid parachute. He fired a flare and soon the choppers landed in front of him. He was picked up by one helicopter and brought back to the base hospital. The other helicopter continued its search for Imtiaz, but abandoned mission as the sun started descending below the horizon. These helicopters were not fit for night flying. Salman remembers thrice coming in severe jet wash during their flight as wingman.

Since Imtiaz was lying down on the other side of the hills, he was not readily visible to the rescue chopper. After some time, he again heard the noise of the helicopters and started shouting as if he could be heard inside the cockpit of that helicopter. The second time, the chopper remained far away from his position as it scanned the area. The noise of the rotating blades of the chopper gradually faded away in the distance. Imtiaz was hit by the reality of no night search or rescue facility at the Masroor Air Base. The thought of spending the night in that wilderness brought shivers to his body and the fear of death occupied his mind. He thought of his new wife, Naheed. She was in the family way with their first child. In desperation he cried and prayed for help from Almighty Allah.

Naheed, wife of Imtiaz, lived in the city of Karachi with her in-laws. Imtiaz would usually return home by evening after completing his duty at the base. After attending a one-dish lunch party that day, she had taken an afternoon nap and then prepared to receive Imtiaz in the evening. When Imtiaz did not return at the usual time, Naheed became concerned. The doorbell rang as she apprised her in-laws that Imtiaz so far had not returned home. After attending the door, her brother-in-law informed her that Wing Commander Sohail, Officer Commanding (OC) of Imtiaz, had come with his wife. The families of No. 19 Squadron with the family of their OC had gone crabbing the day before. Seeing Wing Commander Sohail and his wife casually dressed and gloomy, Naheed ran inside crying that Imtiaz's aircraft had crashed.

She had already been briefed by the wives of the squadron pilots about the Air Force protocol of approaching the family of a pilot whose aircraft had crashed. First, the OC squadron would say that the pilot was missing; next, the OC Wing would declare him injured; and finally, the Base Commander would deliver the sad news of the pilot's death. Zahid Qadeer, another coursemate and buddy of Imtiaz, had accompanied Wing Commander Sohail. He told Naheed that he was stating the truth. The other pilot had been rescued but Imtiaz was missing. The search was called off due to darkness, but would continue the next day with the first light. Naheed half-heartedly believed Zahid and tried to keep her hope alive. She cried and prayed for the life of her husband. Friends and neighbours came to console her.

Shadows lengthened as the sun set behind the hill. Imtiaz was aware that the night search and rescue facility was not available at Masroor. He was reminded of Flight Lieutenant Pervez, who had crashed while ferrying an F-6 aircraft from China. After ejection in the snow-covered mountains of China, Pervez had survived a week before he died of hunger and loss of blood. His body was recovered six months after the crash when the snow melted. In search of shelter, Pervez had dragged himself with a broken leg many miles before succumbing to death. The week-old beard on his face made them believe that he had remained alive for seven days. Finding himself in similar conditions, Imtiaz mentally prepared himself to spend the night and for the indefinite period that lay ahead. He tried to rationalize the entire situation. He had some energy tablets in his survival kit, but he would save them for the worst time that lay ahead.

Back at the base the rescue party gathered around the drawing board. Meteorology squadron had informed them that the wind speed and direction at 15,000 feet at that time over the ejection area was from east to west at 25 knots. Keeping the wind speed in mind, the search copters had scanned the area towards the west of the ejection point. However, when Salman was later interviewed in the hospital, he informed them that the actual wind condition experienced by him was opposite to the wind direction reported by the Met officer. A change in plan to scan the eastern side of the ejection was made by the rescue pilots as they impatiently waited for dawn. Rescue helicopters got airborne at the first light with OC Flying Wing, Group Captain Atta on board.

Imtiaz had concluded that his position in the low lying area was the main reason that the helicopters couldn't locate him. He looked at himself to observe that his left arm was bleeding, his neck and back were badly hurt, and his left ankle had dislocated. Thoughts of death danced around his mind, but he decided not to give up easily. He took out the survival knife from his coverall and cut off a piece of the parachute. He tied the material around his bleeding arm and made a sling to hang around his neck. He gave another cut to the bright red-coloured piece of the parachute and wrapped it around his body so as to be more visible from the air. He grabbed a big stone in his right arm and started dragging himself up the hillock. He kept looking around at the small caves that were spread all over that hilly area. He entered one of these caves to rest after every hour. He was mindful of taking refuge in a cave that was big enough just to hold him. He would sit there facing the open end with his knife in his hand should a wild animal appear to attack.

Sometimes he heard the growling of some animals, but to his good fortune they always remained at a distance. At the break of dawn, he found himself very close to the top of the hillock. He lay there to rest when suddenly he heard the familiar hammering noise that soon turned into the sound of rotating helicopter blades. With all of his energy returning, he relentlessly started to drag himself further upwards to the top of that hillock. Hardly had he reached the top when the roaring helicopter passed overhead. As he looked upwards, he saw someone from the cabin of the helicopter waving at him. He had been spotted! He fainted with joy and let his body lay on the ground. After some time he regained consciousness and heard his name. Someone was calling "Imtiaz!" at the top of his lungs. He shouted back and was soon surrounded by OC Flying and some squadron pilots. He drank some water and lit a cigarette before being carried on a stretcher to the helicopter that had landed some distance from his position.

News of his recovery was immediately transmitted to Masroor Control Tower. Naheed had spent the whole night without sleeping a wink. Her heart sank when she was told that the Base Commander of Masroor was on the line for her. She took the receiver and wept for joy when the Base Commander told her that the helicopters had found Imtiaz alive and that he was on his way to the base. With her in-laws Naheed rushed towards the base.

Imtiaz and Naheed are still happily married with three children. Imtiaz took early retirement as Squadron Leader and is a captain on the Airbus A-380. Salaman retired as Wing Commander and flies for an airline of Pakistan. Javed rose to the rank of Air Marshal before retiring from service.

# Ejected - Gear up Landing!

It was a beautiful afternoon in the spring of 1980. Weather conditions at Masroor Air Base were CAVOK (Clouds and Visibility Okay), meaning it was a great day for flying. I stood behind the hot seat of Duty Air Traffic Controller (DATCO) in the Control Tower sipping a hot cup of tea. A formation of 4 F-6 aircraft of No. 23 squadron with call sign of Abdali Section was inbound from Samungli Air Base. The formation was led by Wing Commander Ilyas Baig who was commanding the No. 23 squadron. My coursemate, Flying Officer Adnan Mazhar, was No. 2; Flight Lieutenant Tahir Afzal was No. 3; and another coursemate of mine, Flying Officer Mazhar Baig, was No. 4 in the formation.

Sonmiani firing range was used for air to ground firing practice by squadrons from other Air Bases as well. No. 23 squadron had flown over 600 kilometres from Samungli Air Base near Quetta. They were to stay at Masroor for the next few days.

It was rush hour for local jet traffic at Masroor Tower. Abdali's formation was adjusted for priority landing over other local traffic. The formation of four came normal on initials and was cleared to land after hearing the base gear check call.

Abdali Leader landed and was about to clear the runway when No. 2 in the formation touched down with gear up raising lot of dust on the concrete surface. When the aircraft reached about 3000 feet down the runway, I heard a big bang and saw a parachute popping out of the landing aircraft and a pilot dangling under a fully blossomed parachute. Standing from behind the hot seat, I recognized the dangling figure about 150 feet above the runway and about 1,500 feet away from my position in the control tower. I identified him as Adnan. I had seen Adnan's name in the flight plan of the formation, but at that time I wasn't sure if he was No. 2 in the formation. However, the sight of his hanging figure made me think about him.

Flying Officer Wali was the Mobile Officer. He was looking towards the landed aircraft of Wing Commander Ilyas Baig. When he turned his head towards the approach path, he suddenly saw an aircraft without gear on short finals. He thought of pulling the red cartridge pin of the auto pistol installed at the threshold of the runway. When pulled, a red cartridge would fire to indicate a go-round to the aircraft on final approach, but Adnan's aircraft had touched down on the runway even before he could fire. The pilot forgot to lower his gear and the Mobile Officer missed. "Whatever can go wrong, will go wrong" - Murphy's Law had kicked in once again.

Today, Adnan still does not know what went wrong. According to him, "I could only see rising dust all around and hear the rumbling noise of metal touching the concrete runway surface." The first thing that came to his mind was the reliability of the Martin Baker ejection seat. He immediately pulled the ejection handle to get out of that dangerous looking cockpit.

Flight Lieutenant Tahir Afzal No. 3 was turning finals and Flying Officer Mazhar No. 4 in the formation had checked the base leg when they saw a parachute popping out from the landed aircraft. They were ordered to go round as the landing runway was blocked. Mazhar, No. 4 in the formation, was flying into Masroor for the first time and had never before landed at Faisal Air Base, a few miles away from Masroor. Luckily, Tahir was an experienced pilot who carried him to the diversion airfield of Faisal Air Base. Many other aircraft were diverted to Faisal on that evening.

The aircraft remained intact and was soon towed off the runway after the engineering staff lowered the landing gear. When the hydraulic power was applied by the engineering staff, the aircraft got up on its wheels like an elephant getting up on its feet. The professional personnel of the Pakistan Air Force comprised of the engineering branch and the ATC got the runway cleared and made it available for all flying activity within an hour of the accident.

Tahir Afzal later embraced martyrdom in a midair collision of mirages. His tragic crash is mentioned in the beginning story of *The Last Salute*.

# "Falcon Blue Leader - Eject!"

### *A MIRACULOUS SURVIVAL*

On a beautiful afternoon in December, 1982, my coursemate Flight Lieutenant Masood Karim took off as "Falcon Blue Leader". He led a formation of two Mirage aircraft from the Sargodha air base. Flight Lieutenant Shahid M. Shigri, though senior in service, flew as his wing man as per the requirement of that planned mission. On ground, they were briefed to fly a strafing and bombing mission over the Laalian firing range. After releasing their weapons on the range, they were to climb up and engage in Air Combat Maneuvres (ACMs). Both pilots recognized this as one of the best flights they had ever flown together. For Masood, it also became his last flight on a fighter jet as he never flew again in those thundering birds. To be a fighter pilot is a dream of millions, but it becomes reality for only a chosen few.

After the ACMs, the two Mirages headed back to base for a full stop landing. As the formation was turning initials at 900 feet above the ground and about a mile short of the landing runway, Masood heard a frantic call on his radio. His No. 2, Flight Lieutenant Shigri, shouted "Falcon Blue Leader. You are on fire - Eject!" When Masood looked inside the cockpit at the instrument panel, the afterburner light was on but all the other instruments showed normal. A second call from Shigri followed immediately: "Leader. You are on fire - Eject!" The Air Traffic Controller relayed the eject call too. The mobile officer also called for Falcon Blue Leader to eject.

Masood in the meantime switched off the afterburner fuel pump. Within the next few seconds, he noticed a slight dip of the nose of the aircraft, and saw his engine parameters winding down. This indicated an engine shutdown. He pushed the air re-light switch. Ahead of him appeared the city of Sargodha and a portion of the base. He initiated a climbing left-hand turn to steer away from the base and the city. He corrected the aircraft attitude for ejection and then reached for the seat pan ejection handle. The seat pan ejection handle, preferred for low level ejections, is installed at the bottom of the seat behind the control column. When Masood pulled the handle, it moved slightly. Expecting a 16-G push into the air, he waited to be thrown out of the cockpit, but - nothing happened!

During these few seconds the aircraft had lost its speed, but its speed then increased as the nose went down in a dive. At that very moment Masood saw the village of Remount Depot in front of him. He continued the turn to the left while gradually pulling up the nose. He again tried to eject. This time, he used the face blind method and grabbed the other ejection handle installed above his head. He pulled it down with both hands - nothing happened. He gave it another strong pull - no joy. He desperately wanted to be out of that falling jet so he pulled down the handle for the third time with all his force. The ejection handle came free. From the corner of his eye he saw the thick steel wire go slipping down like a silver snake. The reliable Martin Baker ejection seat had failed.

Ejection had not worked and the radio was jammed between the ATC, the wingman, and the mobile - all shouting at him to eject. He heard Shigri calling him by name:

"Masood, for God's sake eject now."

Masood transmitted his only call,

"Unable to eject - will force land."

There was no forced landing procedure or any reference to the gliding speed provided by the Mirage-III aircraft emergency procedure checklist. He was just going by the feel of the aircraft, keeping it above the stick shaker speed. The moment he felt the stick shake, he would put the nose down. Masood says he was gliding down at about 340 to 345 knots. Getting close to the ground, he lowered gear and was relieved to see the three green lights confirming the down position of the landing gear.

He maneuvred the aircraft between a row of trees and remembers a soft but positive touchdown. Bushes and trees came rushing towards him at a tremendous speed. The good old T-37 forced landing procedure learned from his days at the Air Force Academy came to his mind: "feet off the rudders, stick to one side, and head down." He never felt the impact of the aircraft being broken by the trees into two pieces. The cockpit broke off to the left while rest of the air frame broke off to the right.

Later, it was discovered that after breaking off from the rear, the cockpit had rolled off to its left side and went dragging for some 200 feet. Masood's left arm had dislocated when it flung out, getting caught under the cockpit. The rear of the aircraft had been on fire during the entire scenario and the fuel came gushing out of the burning aircraft.

With his right hand stuck around the control stick, Masood blacked out for a moment. When he regained consciousness, he noticed a man trying to pull him out of the cockpit. A farmer working in the nearby field had come to rescue him. He was stuck inside with his hand under the cockpit. Masood thought that the aircraft was still intact and on its landing gear. He remembered that two practice bombs and some live gun rounds were still left in the aircraft, and ascertained that the burning aircraft was bound to explode. Masood told his rescuer that the aircraft was going to explode, and inquired if he had a sickle. He then pleaded with the rescuing farmer to cut off his left arm which was stuck under the canopy. The farmer told him not to worry and tried to lift the hot cockpit with both of his hands. When another person working in the fields (a nephew of the farmer) arrived, together they lifted the hot cockpit and pulled out Masood's arm. After pulling him out of the cockpit, the three men ran away from the aircraft. After running only a few steps, Masood heard explosions. He later came to know that the oxygen bottle and gun rounds had exploded. The nephew of the farmer received some splinters in his back. Luckily, they did not go too deep. Masood was put on a cot that had been placed a few hundred yards away from the cockpit. He drifted in and out of consciousness.

During one of his conscious moments, he saw an old village lady covering his body to save him from the exploding bullets. In her simple village accent, she asked him not to worry. Then she prayed to Allah Almighty to save this son, and not to take away another son. Masood later found out that she was the mother of a soldier martyred during the Indo-Pak war of 1971.

Masood fainted again. Upon regaining consciousness, he found Air Commodore Farooq Feroz Khan (F. F. Khan), the Base Commander, holding his head in his lap. F. F. Khan told Masood,

"I am here; do not worry. You will be perfectly fine. No harm can come to you now." Masood was taken to the Sargodha Base Hospital. His left hand sustained multiple compound fractures and burns. After a few days, he was transported in a C-130 aircraft to the main Combined Military Hospital in Rawalpindi. Infected wounds declared him unfit for further flying. After an honourable retirement from the Pakistan Air Force, he started a new chapter of his life. Masood has remained engaged with aviation in various capacities with different airline companies. He now works for the Boeing Company in Seattle.

Masood says that he remained at peace throughout the entire ordeal and did not register any anxiety, fear, or panic. He consistently took every possible action to survive and he kept accepting the unfolding results. He remembers reciting Kalma (holy verses uttered at the time of death) before touching down, believing that his last moments had arrived.

It was later revealed that when he had pulled up the seat pan handle, it had not moved up straight. The attached wire had moved to the side, thereby locking the system. When he went for the face blind ejection, then the steel wire attached to the handle had broken. Later, discovery of a spanner indicated that during the ground maintenance of the ejection seat, the technician had left his spanner behind and this had obstructed the entire ejection system. The life-saving ejection system installed by the Martin Baker Company and the maintenance provided by the Air Force to ensure efficiency of the system had both failed. Skillful handling of a demanding situation and timely actions rescued him that day. Masood simply thinks that the prayers of his parents saved him.

## NOTES OF RECOGNITION FROM MASOOD KARIM

The old gentleman who reached the aircraft through the burning fuel was a retired firefighter from the base. He was cutting fodder in the fields when he saw the aircraft coming down in flames towards him. With him were his nephew and his eighteen-year-old grandson. As the aircraft was heading straight for them, they ran to either side. The retired firefighter and his nephew went to the left of the winding track while the grandson went to the right. The young boy received over eighty percent burns to his body and passed away on the third day after the crash. The old firefighter kept throwing green fodder on the burning fuel to save Masood without knowing the fate of his grandson. Masood will always remember them.

He remembers the love and affection given to him by the officers and families at the Sargodha Air Force Base. Masood will always remain grateful to them.

The Base Commander, Air Commodore F. F. Khan, was attending a funeral service at Sargodha Air Force College when he was informed of the crash. After confirming the position of the crash site, he rushed his staff car through the fields and uneven tracks, beating even the rescue helicopter. F. F. Khan, a veteran of the Indo-Pak war, later commanded the Pakistan Air Force as Air Chief Marshal until his appointment as Chairman - Joint Chief of Staff.

Flight Lieutenant Shigri lived a full life. He was a courageous person with the wits of a genuine fighter pilot and commander. He had a caring heart of love and affection, and was devoted to the country and the Air Force. He served in a number of critical and prestigious positions, especially in the area of air defence systems. He attained the rank of Air Commodore before dying in a road accident when a truck rammed into his car.

The Air Force tenure for Masood was short, his dream career being short-lived, but he treasures the most profound memories of a beautiful life. The brothers of 65th G.D. (P.) course, seniors and juniors in Lower Topa and Risalpur Academies, friends of No. 11 and No. 5 Squadrons, worthy instructors (then) Flight Lieutenant Hamid (Glider), Flight Lieutenant Shabbir/ Flight Lieutenant Assad Mehmood (MFI-17), Flight Lieutenant Akram, and Flying Officer Aqeel (T-37), Flight Lieutenant Muddassir (FT-5), Flight Lieutenant Pervaiz Khan (F-6), instructors of No. 9 Operational Conversion Unit, and instructors of F-6 and Mirage Combat Commander School, will always remain an integral part of his life. Long live the Pakistan Air Force.

*Zahid Malik*

*Masood Karim*

*Sqn. Ldr. Imtiaz Ahmed*

*Air Cdr. Amjad Bashir*

*From Left: Abbas, Mohajir, Rehman, Mazhar
and Tahir Afzal sitting extreme right*

*Adnan and Nusrat*

# Adventures of AVM Abbas Mirza

Air Vice Marshal (AVM) Abbas Mirza served the PAF at various important positions. He carries the rich experience of 4000 plus hours of flying various single and multi-engine fighter aircraft including F16, MIRAGE, F104, F86, Hunter, MIG21and MIG19. He commanded the prestigious Combat Commanders School (CCS) from 1980 to 1982 and commanded the PAF Base Shorekot from 1985 to 1987. From 1987 to 1989, he remained Assistant Chief of the Air Staff, Flight Safety. He was Air Officer Commanding, Northern Air Command from 1989 to 1992 and served as Inspector General of the Air Force from 1992 before retiring from the Air Force in 1994.

After retirement he was appointed as Ambassador of Pakistan to Myanmar and Vietnam, where he served from 1994 to 1996. AVM Mirza now lives in Vancouver with his wife Rukhsana.

I had several friendly meetings with AVM Mirza in Vancouver during which we remembered the good old Air Force days, talked about politics in Pakistan, and discussed my book, *The Last Salute*. One late afternoon, after an early supper at a restaurant in West Vancouver, he recounted his experience of two ejections and of reaching Mach 2 speed while flying the F-104 Star Fighter aircraft. I observed that these incidents sounded attractive for my book. When he graciously agreed to narrate them, I immediately took out my cell phone and recorded our conversation.

AVM Mirza is mentioned in two other chapters of this book: first when I seek guidance from him on the occasion of leaving the Pakistan Air Force; and second he becomes a part of the story as the President of the Board of Inquiry in the crash of General Zia-Ul-Haq, assassinated President of Pakistan.

He ejected once from the F-86 aircraft fitted with a C2 seat having a minimum limit of 250 feet above the ground and 100 knots of speed for a successful ejection. The second ejection took him out of the cockpit of the F-6 aircraft while using the Chinese ejection seat.

# "Mobile 211- Ejecting!"

On the 3rd of June, 1967, at the start of the Arab-Israeli War, Abbas Mirza, who was at that time a Flight Lieutenant, had a little quarrel with his friend Flight Lieutenant Aman-Ullah over flying the test mission of an F-86 aircraft. As young eagles, they often fought to grab every opportunity of getting airborne.

Mirza won the argument and Aman-Ullah agreed to perform the duties of the Mobile Officer. He would work in a Mobile hut, which is a small glass house close to the threshold of the landing runway. Equipped with radio transmitters and manned by an operational pilot who provides help from the ground to the airborne aircraft in any emergency, the Mobile hut is a mini control tower.

They were posted in No. 26 Squadron at Peshawar Air Base as instructors on the F-86 aircraft. The maintenance squadron cleared an overstressed F-86 aircraft following a major overhaul. It was awaiting a test flight known as the FCF (Functional Check Flight). Fighter pilots enjoyed flying the test flights as this duty provided the rare opportunity of flying a clean aircraft. The absence of extra fuel tanks and weapons increased the maneuverability of the aircraft. The pleasure of flying a sleek machine remained higher than the dangers associated with the handling of a recently repaired aircraft.

Call sign '211' - Mirza - taxied out on a sunny day, perfect for flying, although a gusty wind of about 15 knots prevailed around the airfield. After takeoff, he carried out a low-level straight run at 200 feet above the ground in front of the mobile at 400 knots to show off and to make his buddy Aman-Ullah jealous. Immediately after, he pulled up in to a lazy vertical roll, topping out at around 10,000 feet before climbing on to 20,000 feet to begin the entire required tests which progressed normally. He could visualize

Aman-Ullah envying him. Until today, they are great buddies who always enjoyed their flying. Aman-Ullah, a superb pilot in his own right, was cited with shooting down at least two Indian aircraft. He retired from the Air Force after rising to the rank of Air Commodore.

At about 20,000 to 21,000 feet he reduced speed to 105 knots to check the stalling characteristics in the last part of the exercise before putting the aircraft into a spin. When the speed dropped to 105 knots, the aircraft started to buffet before stalling. When he pushed the stick forward to recover out of the stall, he then found that it was stuck in the full back position into his stomach. Unable to push the stick forward, he tried the alternate trim. His efforts were fruitless, and the aircraft continued to buffet with its nose going up in high attitude.

He called the Mobile Officer to inform him about the emergency, and explained that the aircraft was about to enter the spin. From the Mobile hut Aman-Ullah advised Mirza to check the hydraulic pressures. Finding the hydraulic pressures normal, he pulled the alternate handle. That action raised the pressure to 4000 PSI, but nothing happened to the control column. Meanwhile, the aircraft entered into a spin and his fall towards the ground increased at a rapid speed. He applied the opposite rudder to come out of the spin, but it didn't stop. Recovery out of a spin demanded application of the opposite rudder and pushing the stick to its full forward position. Nothing worked.

Spinning down rapidly, trapped behind the control stick, he continued struggling with the control column to no avail. Again, he called Mobile:

"Mobile; unable to recover from spin, control column stuck in full back position."

He repeatedly heard the frantic calls of Aman-Ullah,

"211 Eject."— "211 Eject."

Mirza kept trying to recover. But when he looked at the altimeter passing through 10,000 feet, he called:

"Mobile - 211 ejecting."

He followed the proper ejection procedure, which he had practiced dry, many times before, on the ground. This procedure required him to follow a two-phase process: first, jettisoning the canopy; and then, firing the seat.

He lowered his head to avoid being hit by the canopy and then pulled the trigger on the right side of his seat. When the canopy jettisoned, he straightened up again, positioned his head fully back onto the headrest, and stretched his back as much as possible to avoid stress fracture. A glance at the altimeter revealed that he was passing 7000 feet. He squeezed the ejection trigger that immediately fired the seat out of the cockpit. Luckily, none of his body parts touched the fuselage or the tail when he was thrown tumbling out of the cockpit.

The moment he came out of the cockpit, the wind removed the helmet from his head to leave it strapped around his neck. He felt a positive tug, looked up, and saw the chute fully blossomed. After putting the helmet back onto his head, he tried to stabilize the chute that had sharply oscillated because of the strong wind. He put on the oxygen mask; activated the emergency oxygen bottle hanging on his left side; and tried to control the swing of the parachute that had turned violent by then. He thought the swing might go beyond vertical, making him land on the chute itself.

Oscillation grew stronger to about 15 to 20 degrees on either side. Looking down later, he could see the village below and people looking upwards towards him. Fear of hitting someone during landing worried him. Fortunately, he missed them all, hit a mud wall, and landed with a big thud in front of a buffalo. The buffalo was more scared than Mirza and it jumped away without hurting him. It took him about ten minutes to hit the ground after ejecting from around 7000 feet. The villagers put him on a cot and gave him

VIP treatment in a display of great hospitality. He drank a lot of milk before being picked up by the Search and Rescue helicopter. Severe shooting pain arose in his right ankle, which was later confirmed to be broken. He remained in the hospital nursing his only injury for twenty days.

When questioned about his feelings and fears during the emergency, AVM Mirza became philosophical. He firmly believed in the theory of time dilation. He explained it as a difference in the elapsed time of an event measured by observers at two different locations. Mirza believed that his brain worked at an extraordinary speed during this emergency because of the pressure he was under. He performed the necessary actions very quickly in a short time that appeared as an eternity to him. However, when listening to his tape-recorded conversation, he realized that it took less than a minute from his call of entering into a spin to his call of ejection. Throughout the ordeal, he remained focused on dealing with the emergency. Feelings for any loved ones or fear of death had never even crossed his mind.

This emergency was not outlined in the emergency procedures, but professionalism and training took over and action was taken to try and recover with the help of ground control. There was no time to think of anything else. The possibility of what might have happened occurs much later when one is safe and sound and then one thanks the Almighty for his protection.

# Frightening Dream

Rukhsana Mirza had a strange dream which acted as an early warning to real life events that would occur a few days later. She was in Karachi with her mother while her husband, Abbas Mirza, then a Squadron Leader and Flight Commander in 23 Squadron, was based in Sargodha flying the F-6 aircraft (the Chinese version of the MIG-19 Farmer). The F-6 had recently beaten the Starfighter F-104 in a race to 30,000 feet before the Starfighter F-104 took over. Pilots considered the F-6 a real live-wire thrill to fly.

The night before leaving to join her husband, Rukhsana had a frightening and stunning dream. In the dream, she recalls Wing Commander Carapiet, Officer Commanding (OC) Flying in Sargodha, calling to tell her that Abbas had ejected from an F-6 close to the ground. The chute had failed to open, and he hadn't survived. Worried, she narrated the dream to her mother, who advised Rukhsana to pray the Ayat al Kursi (verses from the Holy Quran) and give Sadka (Charity), which she promptly did. Rukhsana then put this dream behind her and left to join her husband in Sargodha.

A few days later Mirza was readying himself for a Functional Flight Check (FCF) mission. The date was December 7th, 1974, the anniversary of the Japanese attack against Pearl Harbor. It was also on December 7th, 1961 that Mirza had graduated as a pilot from Craig Air Force Base in Alabama. Interestingly, Mirza's first ejection was on June 3rd, 1967, the day of the start of the Arab-Israeli Six-Day War. To add to the list of coincidences, Amanullah, Mirza's close friend who was the Mobile Officer in Peshawar the day Mirza ejected the first time, had performed as his Squadron-Commander at that time. Unfortunately, Amanullah had a back injury from his own recent ejection, which had taken place while the airplane was inverted and in rapid descent. Injury had placed him on non-flying status.

December 7th, 1974 dawned bright and sunny - one of those beautiful winter days in the heart of Pakistan. The pleasure of the moment was enhanced by the fact that the F-6 Mirza was to fly waited for him without extra fuel tanks and weapons in a "clean configuration". This helped keep him alive after the accident!

Squadron Leader Abbas Mirza stepped into the cockpit of the F-6 and carried out his preflight routine, including the ejection procedure as was his habit. The F-6 that Mirza was flying had the old Chinese ejection seat which had a safe ejection limit of 600 feet above the ground level (AGL) and 450 kilometres per hour (kph). These seats were later replaced by the Martin Baker "zero-zero" seats, which meant you could safely eject from them while the aircraft was on the ground.

There were two methods of ejection: first, by pulling on the face blind which initially jettisoned the canopy and then fired the seat. This was the preferred method as it entailed only one action by the pilot and was quicker than the second method, which was a more complicated multi-step process: first, jettison the canopy by pulling on the ejection seat lever; second, place the head against the headrest; third, squeeze the trigger to fire the seat while keeping the back straight. This method, which took just a bit longer, was preferred when time was not a factor. On one occasion the face blind had malfunctioned and the pilot had been unable to eject. Mirza always practiced the second method in his pre-flight checks.

After conducting a normal test flight, he asked the control tower for joining instructions. From the tower, Fareed Bilgrami, a Pilot Officer at that time, passed on the joining instructions for Runway 14. Mirza came back normal on initials at 1,500 feet above the ground a couple of miles short abeam the landing runway and pitched out. Pitchout, a maneuvre at circuit altitude, is conducted by putting a 60 degree bank at about one third the initial length of the landing runway. This maneuvre brings the jet aircraft on the inner downwind position, thereby reducing speed to lower the landing gear before turning onto the base leg.

The F-6 aircraft had a bleed band issue as explained earlier. As Mirza brought the throttles below 9,500 rpm and put the speed brakes out to slow down from 700 kph to 500 kph (the necessary speed for lowering the landing gear), he heard a loud rumbling noise. Instantly glancing at the rpm and EGT (exhaust gas temperature) gauges he noticed that both engines had stagnated at around 6,500 rpm to 7000 rpm, and the EGTs had shot up to 900 degrees centigrade. Reckoning on the symptoms of an engine compressor stall he called on the radio, "Fox 66 double engine stall shutting down left engine and restarting." Inside the Control Tower, Pilot

Officer Fareed Bilgrami got a shock when he heard the radio call. The voice was cool and calm - too calm for the emergency he knew was impending. Recognizing the seriousness of the situation, he jumped out of his seat and pressed the crash bell. While Mirza was battling the emergency, the crash and rescue operation had already been initiated by mobilizing the fire-fighting services and the rescue helicopter.

Inside the cockpit, Mirza shut down the left engine and had a successful relight, but as he pushed the throttle up, the engine stalled again. He continuously tried to keep the aircraft flying above the safe ejection seat limit. He lowered the nose and pushed the speed brakes in to maintain 450 kph. All of this was happening at a frantic pace but to Mirza, as he had felt in his earlier ejection, every move he made was in real SLOW motion as if time had stopped. In fact, the time between the first call and the last was probably no more than 30 to 40 seconds. In extreme situations of life and death, people have been known to experience time dilation - an evolutionary response to heighten alertness and judgment that effectively maximizes chances of survival.

The engine stalled again. Abbas called out to mobile, "Restart successful but stalled again. Fox 66 ejecting..." The last he saw on the altimeter was 800 ft and 450 kph right at the edge of the seat envelope. He knew it was going to be touch and go.

With no time to spare, Mirza chose the more reliable but also more complicated multi-step ejection process: he lowered his head, jettisoned the canopy, put his head back, kept his back straight, and fired the seat. He had trained and rehearsed this method before every sortie, including this one. Tumbling out of the cockpit, Mirza bundled himself up to try and absorb the shock of hitting the ground if the chute did not open, and then for the first time it dawned on him that he might not make it. Fortunately, the chute blossomed fully a few feet above the ground, and a couple of swings later he landed with a heavy thud in a freshly plowed field with absolutely no injuries. Mirza was in the process of gathering his chute when the rescue helicopter with the Base Commander aboard came to pick him up.

On the ground Bilgrami heard the call. He saw the canopy jettison and the seat leave the aircraft. He watched and waited to see the chute blossom, but saw only the chute streaming without opening fully as it fell below the tree line. Bilgrami, while narrating this event from Australia, told me that he was highly impressed by the professional way Mirza had handled the emergency: "There was no hint of panic or stress in all of Mirza's calls." The word went out that Mirza had ejected too late and the chute had not opened fully.

In the meantime, the rescue helicopter with the Base Commander Air Commodore Jamal Khan (later Air Chief Marshal and Chief of the Air Staff) was getting airborne.

At Mirza's home, Rukhsana received a call from Wing Commander Carapiet telling her - mimicking exactly what had transpired in her dream a few days earlier - Abbas had ejected very close to the ground. Not knowing at that moment whether he had survived, and having received reports that he may not have made it, Carapiet nonetheless tried to assure Rukhsana: "Don't worry, he has ejected, and was last seen flushing some partridges from the area." Mirza and Carapiet were avid hunters and often went out together for partridge shoots.

Rukhsana ran to tell her mother-in-law, Mirza's mother, what had happened. She immediately asked Rukhsana to recite verses from the Holy Quran and to place her faith in the Almighty. The dream was a premonition for sure, except for the very last detail: her husband survived. He was taken to the local hospital for a few medical checks and then released to go home. He flew again the very next day and continued to fly without mishap for the next 20 years. Was it the 'Sadka' (charity money given by Rukhsana) and the prayers that saved Mirza? Rukhsana firmly believes so. Mirza and Rukhsana remain happily married to this day.

# The Order of the Starfighter — F-104

The F-104 Starfighter is a beautiful aircraft that looks more like a rocket than an airplane. It epitomizes speed through its radical design and was nicknamed the "missile with a man in it". Conceived by Clarence "Kelly" Johnson in the Skunk Works facilities in California and Nevada, the F-104 first flew on February 17th, 1956. Over a dozen countries, including member nations of NATO, eventually had the F-104 in their inventory. The Starfighter was designed to intercept high flying Soviet bombers in the Cold War era. It was the first and only Mach 2 aircraft that held both the world speed and altitude records simultaneously. Interestingly, sixty years after its first flight the F-104 is still in service and its latest mission is to launch small commercial satellites into orbit.

Pilot Officer Abbas Mirza had returned from his flight training in the USA in 1963 and was posted to No. 11 Squadron in Sargodha under the command of Wing Commander Anwar Shamim, who later became the Chief of the Air Staff (CAS). Wing Commander M.M. Alam, the legendary ace pilot who shot down five Indian aircraft in a single mission in the 1965 Indo-Pak war, took over from Shamim. Mirza had the privilege to fly and train under such brilliant pilots and leaders.

In 1964, Mirza was promoted to the rank of Flying Officer and posted to No. 9 squadron "The Griffins" under Wing Commander Jamal A. Khan, later the CAS. Coincidentally, Jamal was the Base Commander who would later recover Abbas after his ejection from an F-6 aircraft in 1974.

For young Mirza, it was a singular honour to be selected to fly the F-104 Starfighter. He was also fortunate to operate the F-104 both in the 1965 and 1971 air campaigns against India. In 1965 he was credited, along with then Wing Commander Hakimullah, with the forced landing of an Indian Gnat aircraft at Pasrur airfield in Pakistan. Hakimullah later commanded the Pakistan Air Force.

The term Mach number was coined by Jacob Ackeret, a Swiss aeronautical engineer. Jacob dedicated the term "Mach" in honour of the Austrian physicist and philosopher, Ernest Mach, for his study of shock waves. Shock waves are generated when an object flies close to the speed of sound and the Mach number is a quantity defining the speed of sound. Mach 1 is equal to the speed of sound. The speed of sound is directly affected by the temperature and density of the medium through which it travels.

Preparation for the Mach 2 mission begins at least a day prior to the flight. The F-104 has to be stripped of all external stores and rails so that the aircraft is in a "clean" configuration. The meteorological office is contacted to calculate the height of the tropopause on the day of the flight. The tropopause is the boundary between the troposphere and the stratosphere. The tropopause is where the outside air temperature is lowest. The tropopause generally lies between 34,000 feet and 62,000 feet, depending on latitude and season. Finding the tropopause is important, as air friction causes temperature to rise and the engine air inlet temperature can go beyond 100 degrees centigrade. The F-104 has a limit of 100 degrees on its engine inlet temperature. If the temperature increases beyond 100 degrees and Mach 2 has not been attained, the mission has to be aborted.

Another important requirement is the correct movement of the shock cones during the flight. The F-104 has one shock cone located at the entrance of each air intake. The shock cones work in conjunction with the Mach number beyond Mach 1.2. The function of the shock cones is to slow down the air from supersonic speed to subsonic speed before it enters the engine. Failure of the shock cones leads to a catastrophic engine compressor stall. If the shock cones do not correspond to the Mach number, the mission has to be aborted.

The third factor is to monitor engine revs per minute (rpm) as the aircraft accelerates beyond 1.6 Mach. As the engine air inlet temperature increases, the density of the air reduces. To compensate for this reduction, the engine rpm automatically increases to 103.2%. This is known as T2 reset. If T2 reset does not occur, the mission has to be aborted.

One of the rites of passage for joining pilots was to fly a Mach 2 mission. This milestone was looked forward to by all pilots as a really fun ride. The Mach 2 flight was not an everyday event as it required special planning and aircraft configuration as described earlier. Normal operational training sorties rarely went beyond Mach 1.2.

On a clear winter day in 1964, Mirza calculated the tropopause and went over the emergency procedures for shock cone and T2 reset failures along with his chase pilot Wing Commander Middlecoat. Also discussed was the procedure for deceleration from Mach 2 to Mach 1.6. Middlecoat cautioned Mirza not to exceed Mach 2 or 50,000 feet. Flight above 50,000 feet requires pressure suits. On this flight, they would not be wearing pressure suits. The mission called for a full afterburner climb at Mach 0.9 to the tropopause which was at 37,000 feet on that day with an outside temperature of minus 55 degrees Celsius. After levelling off, the formation would proceed to the farthest end of the supersonic corridor as the Mach 2 run takes up a lot of airspace. The climb to the tropopause alone was exhilarating. A kick in the back side confirmed the lighting of the afterburner to start the takeoff. This was followed by a very steep climb angle. Mirza had to make a determined effort not to go supersonic during the climb. After levelling off in less than two minutes from brake release, Middlecoat went over the essentials again: shock cone movement, inlet air temperature, and T2 reset.

Upon reaching the designated area Mirza called for full afterburner and they were off. He remembers the instant acceleration and being pushed back in his seat. Middlecoat called out to maintain level flight as any rate of climb would extend the time taken to reach Mach 2. Mirza found that this was a challenge as the F-104 wanted to climb like a horse pulling at the reins. Pushing the stick forward and using the trim button extensively, Mirza concentrated on flying level. Events were happening rapidly, and already they were crossing Mach 1.2. When

Middlecoat called out "shock cone check", Mirza replied in the affirmative and the mission was a go. The Mach number was increasing rapidly and soon they were at 1.6. Mirza glanced inside and checked the engine air inlet temperature which had risen from minus 55 to 90 degrees Celsius. T2 reset would be occurring soon. Middlecoat's voice came over the earphone to confirm T2 reset and there it was! Rpm 103.2%! The mission could continue to Mach 2. Mirza was fully occupied now, but he took time to look outside and was amazed to see how fast the ground below was moving. Looking down at high altitude, normally the ground seems to stand still. But there was a lot to do inside the cockpit. Mirza, looking at the Mach number, saw the needle creeping towards Mach 2 and then quickly reaching Mach 2! He was flying at 1,288 knots or 1,483 kph. Faster than a speeding bullet and twice the speed of sound! Middlecoat immediately called for the deceleration maneuvre. Mirza pulled the throttle out of afterburner, and then put the F-104 into a steep climbing turn to reduce speed below Mach 1.6. At that point the speed brakes could be used to slow down further. Use of speed brakes above 1.6 is not permitted as a severe nose down pitch movement can cause a compressor stall. Mirza glanced at the altimeter and saw it crossing 47,000. The Mach number was just below 1.6 so he called for speed brakes, reduced rpm, and simultaneously pushed the nose down to stay below 50,000 feet. Mirza found himself breathing heavily after all the adrenaline and the rapid sequence of events. It had been a truly unique, once-in-a-lifetime ride and Mirza found himself smiling inside his oxygen mask.

Upon landing, Mirza was greeted by his squadron mates and doused with a bucket of water! Even the cold water did nothing to dampen Mirza's feeling of elation. Later, in the squadron party that followed, he was presented "The Order of the Starfighter". This certificate is given to all those who have had the privilege of flying at Mach 2. The certificate has found a special place of recognition in the study of his home in Islamabad.

*AVM Abbas Mirza*

*Fareed Bilgrami*

*AVM Abbas Mirza*

*Abbas Mirza & Nusrat*

*Mrs. Rukhsana Mirza &*
*Shaheen Nusrat*

# Chapter Nine
## Flights to Heaven

There are several types of martyrs in Islam. A Hadees (Sayings of Prophet) of Bokhari states, "Whoever is killed while protecting his property is a martyr." Martyrdom also applies to all those who die in the line of duty.

## Crash of Sherdil Leader!

Four T-37 aircraft with the call sign of the Sherdil (Heart of Lion) formation performed aerobatics at every graduation parade at the Risalpur Academy. They flew in closed box or diamond formation performing low-level maneuvres over the parade ground of the Academy. Many major Air Forces of the world have specified pilots to perform only in the aerobatic teams. They also practice with special planes modified for better engine response and more effective flight controls.

In contrast, the Sherdil formation of the PAF was comprised of regular Instructor Pilots. They performed normal instructional duties during regular working hours and practiced aerobatics in the evening. They flew regular T-37 trainer aircraft which had not been adjusted to give better engine response or more effective flight controls.

Sherdil (Heart of the Lion) Leader, Flight Lieutenant Syed Alamdar Hussain was a true lionhearted son of the Air Force. He embraced martyrdom in one of the most tragic crashes in the history of the Air Force. Flight Lieutenant Irfan Masum was a part of the Sherdil formation, flying as left wing man when Alamdar crashed. Irfan, from 56th G.D.(P.) course, had the unique distinction of twice holding the highest appointment of Wing Under Officer as a Flight Cadet: once in Lower Topa and again at Rislapur Academy. He was the instructor of my roommate Asif Aziz Shah who, as a Flight Cadet, also became the Wing Under Officer in Risalpur and earned the best pilot trophy. Asif also crashed in a tragic accident mentioned later in this book. Irfan Masum was awarded Tamgha-e-Basalat during his tour of duty as an instructor pilot at Risalpur. He commanded No. 8 Squadron of the Mirage aircraft before taking voluntary retirement as Wing Commander. I contacted Irfan Masum thirty-six years after the crash to find out the details. The next day he sent a detailed description of the accident.

Flight Lieutenant Akhter Pervez was a close buddy of the Sherdil Leader and they together had shared many interesting moments of life. When I talked to him about Alamdar, he too sent the story of his association with the Sherdil leader. Akhter retired from the service after reaching the rank of Air Commodore.

Flight Lieutenant Alamdar graduated with the 54th G.D.(P.) Course. He held the highest appointment of Wing Under Officer of his course and earned the prestigious 'Sword of Honour' award. The presiding officer of that graduation parade was none other than the then Prime Minister of Pakistan, Mr. Zulfqar Ali Bhutto. The Prime Minister was so impressed with this young and dynamic Flight Cadet leading the parade that he broke all norms of protocol and hugged Alamdar after presenting him the coveted Sword of Honour. Alamdar graduated from the Risalpur Academy on the 8th of October, 1972 as a pilot officer. Six years later, he gave his life in the line of duty on the premises of the same academy.

After graduating from the Fighter Instructor School (FIS) course in 1976, Alamdar became an instructor in the Basic Flight Training (BFT) squadron of T-37 aircraft. He soon became a part of the prestigious team of 'Sherdil' pilots who performed aerobatics during the graduation parade ceremonies of the academy. He started in No. 3 position as left wing man of the Sherdil team. He later became the leader of the Sherdil formation, a position he upheld until the time of his fatal crash. He was the most handsome, happiest, and well-dressed fighter pilot instructor during our time in the academy. I remember, as Flight Cadets at Risalpur, we looked for excuses to get close to him. He was a living legend. We usually saw him on the flight lines or sometimes in the cadets' mess. He was a role model for all the aspiring fighter pilots, and we loved and respected him from the bottom of our hearts.

The Sherdils started their maneuvres by approaching the parade square tucked in the line astern position (slotted one behind the other) at 250 feet above ground level. From the line astern position they joined in the diamond formation as they pulled up for a loop in front of the audience. After completing the loop, the formation executed a cloverleaf maneuvre to the left followed by a positioning wingover to set up for a steep turn. After the steep turn, another positioning wingover led to a barrel roll. After the barrel roll, they pulled up together for a loop and performed the most exciting maneuvre of the show - the 'bomb burst'. The bomb burst occurs when all four aircraft pass the exact vertical position on the way down from a loop with the nose pointing down. Then each member rotates the entire aircraft from nose to tail axis and departs in four different directions from overhead the parade ground. They pull out individually with recovery heights of approximately 200 feet. This appears like four splinters flying out in four different directions after the explosion of a bomb. The tails of the four aircraft throughout the maneuvres emit different coloured smoke.

On the 8th of October, 1978, the day of the crash, the following four pilots formed the Sherdil formation:

Sherdil Leader: Flight Lieutenant Syed Alamdar Hussain

Sherdil 2: Flight Lieutenant Shahid Nisar (right wing)

Sherdil 3: Flight Lieutenant Irfan Masum (left wing)

Sherdil 4: Flight Lieutenant Tasneem Muzaffar (slot behind the leader)

All four pilots of the aerobatic team, after finishing normal instructional flying, met for the preflight briefing on that fateful day. Their experience of flying together for two years kept the briefing short. They knew well the routine and the emergency drill. The four T-37 aircraft took off to the north of the airfield to practice first at a higher altitude.

Flight Lieutenant Akhtar Pervez was playing tennis on the lawn of the officers' mess with some other pilots of the squadron. Even with thousands of flying hours under their belts, they could not resist pausing to look up at their friends flying overhead in formation. Akhtar always had an uneasy feeling when he saw them in the closed box position. He thought the wing men were too close in keeping the integrity of the box. The slot man behind the leader kept a tight position from within a few feet. Akhtar had noticed earlier that Alamdar's right hand fingers and palm carried rough marks on the skin. When he asked Alamdar about this, Alamdar responded that the calluses had formed from the pressure of holding the control stick during the maneuvres. He had to pull back particularly hard during the steep turns. This countered the pressures created by interacting with the aerodynamic forces of his tail-plane and the canopy-bubble of his slot man. Akhtar had urged Alamdar to open up his team in the box formation. But Alamdar was confident about the skills of his team.

After training at high-level, Alamdar radioed his team to continue for a proper rehearsal over the parade ground. Flight Lieutenant Shahid, number 2; Flight Lieutenant Irfan, number 3; and Flight Lieutenant Tasneem, number 4 followed their leader in the astern positions as they descended to 250 feet. From the line astern position they joined in diamond formation while pulling up for the loop and carried out the cloverleaf maneuvre without any problem. During the positioning wingover to carry out the steep turn, Flight Lieutenant Irfan from the left wing position saw in his peripheral vision that the nose of the aircraft of Flight Lieutenant Tasneem from the number 4 position had come closer to the tail of Sherdil Leader. Irfan gave a call saying, "Tasneem, get back a little." Slot coming forward could disturb the airflow under the elevators of the leader and potentially result in the loss of back pressure that he was holding with the control stick. Tasneem immediately adjusted his position behind the leader.

Sherdil Leader radioed "back pressure" as the formation was settling down in the steep turn. It signaled to his formation that he was going to pull g's for stabilizing in the level steep turn at 250 feet. According to Irfan, all appeared normal until that point - then something strange happened. During the steep turn, they experienced a huge bump like one in turbulence. The bump was very strong, resulting in throwing No. 2 (F/Lt. Shahid on the right wing) and No. 3 (F/Lt. Irfan on the left wing) away and above the aircraft of the Sherdil Leader. They lost sight of the leader and the slot. Irfan and Shahid both radioed that they were breaking off.

Shortly after breaking off safely, the Air Traffic Control Tower made a radio call that one Sherdil had crashed near the Mobile of runway 27. Not knowing who that unfortunate aircraft was, No. 3 (Irfan) after some time radioed the Sherdils for check-in. The check-in calls came from No. 2 (Shahid), No. 3 (Irfan), and No. 4 (Tasneem). Absence of a response from the Sherdil leader confirmed his crash.

In the officers' mess at the tennis lawns, Flight Lieutenant Akhtar noticed the Flag Cars speeding towards the technical area gate that led to the runway. Prompted by an unknown fear, he dumped his tennis racquet and ran towards the road. As he reached the road, he saw three aircraft turning initials for Runway 27. His heart sank; he knew that one of the 'Sherdils' - one of his buddies - had gone down. With prayers on his lips he dialed the Air Traffic Control to find out that his friend Alamdar had crashed during the steep turn. He remembered the hard skin in the right hand of Alamdar. There wasn't any margin for error. The low altitude had sealed all chances of ejection.

The remaining Sherdils did not exchange any further calls and recovered independently. All three Sherdils landed back, not knowing the fate of their leader. And none dared to ask on the radio as they feared the worst. They came to know after landing that Flight Lieutenant Alamdar had embraced martyrdom. The 'back pressure' call during the steep turn remained the last words of the Sherdil leader.

The inquiry report revealed the presence of a crack and a red mark on the upper portion of the glass canopy of the aircraft of No. 4 (slot), Flight Lieutenant Tasneem. That red mark was the red paint of the elevator of Alamdar's aircraft. It was perhaps a minor soft contact, but it broke the elevator control surface. During the steep turn the elevators deflect (upwards) under at least 2 g's to preserve height in the steep turn. Any external force, no matter how small, would break the elevators or at least damage them. With no elevator control, Alamdar could do nothing, and with some 60 degrees bank, there was no way to stop the descent that set in immediately after the elevators broke. As the bank continued to increase the aircraft was taken to an inverted position. At 250 feet above the ground, Alamdar probably hit the soil before thinking of any escaping action.

According to Flight Lieutenant Tasneem, the leader's plane suddenly started sitting on him and he had to bunt his plane down to avoid touching the leader's tail. However, since he couldn't continue bunting down as the formation was only 250 feet from the ground, he had to bunt and simultaneously break off or he too would have gone with the leader. In doing so, the canopy of Tasneem touched the elevator of the leader's plane.

How the two aircraft touched each other became a necessary question. There appeared two possibilities: First, a sudden loss of thrust of the leader's engine could have rammed the slot into him. Second, a sudden loss or release of two g's back pressure could have done the same. Squadron Leader Qaiser Hussain, Alamdar's elder brother, commanded No. 1 BFT Squadron at the time of the crash. Pilots of the Sherdil team were already dear to him even before the crash. Later, they became even dearer as he saw Alamdar in all of them. Squadron Leader Qaiser, before retiring from service, rose to the rank of Air Marshal and to the chair of the vice Chief of the Air Force. On each of his promotions Irfan called Qaiser to congratulate him. Each time Qaiser responded with the same answer: "Irfan, I am reaping what was actually meant for Alamdar." In that reply is the greatness of Alamdar.

Flight Lieutenant Shahid Nisar, No. 2 in the Sherdil formation, took over as leader of the Sherdils. While on deputation to Jordan, he established a 'Sherdil'-style aerobatic formation team for the King Hussain Air College. He rose to the rank of Air vice-Marshal and performed as Deputy Chief of the Air Staff (DCAS) Evaluation and Logistics before retiring from the service.

Flight Lieutenant Tasneem No. 4 (slot), whose canopy hit the elevator of Alamdar, left the service after reaching the rank of Squadron Leader. He joined a commercial airline.

## AFTER THE CRASH

Keeping in view the emotional attachment among the pilots of the Sherdil formation and the graduation parade few days later, the Air Force authorities decided not to permit the Sherdil pilots to attend the funeral of Alamdar. To this day members of the Sherdil formation regret with heavy hearts not attending the funeral. However, Alamdar was buried with proper honour awarded by the Air Force contingent that accompanied the dead body to his hometown in Parachinar.

According to Air vice-Marshal Shahid Nisar, the next day after the crash he was called by the Commandant Air Commodore Athar Bokhari and asked to place another pilot in the cockpit. This idea was dropped when Shahid pointed to the possibility of losing two pilots instead of one. Moreover, if the other pilot reacted in a tense situation, then this would cause further confusion of struggle on the controls. AVM Shahid added that on the final day of the parade, Irfan Masum had engine flameout while they were orbiting minutes before the final display. Irfan was so calm in reporting the flameout on manual frequency that Shahid for a second thought it to be a joke. But it was real. Irfan landed through a straight in approach on runway 27. He rejoined the formation after getting airborne on the stand by an aircraft parked at the operational readiness platform (ORP) of runway 09. Irfan was just in time for the final display that was smoothly conducted by the Sherdil formation at the graduation ceremony of 66th and 4th Supplementary G.D.(P.) courses.

## SOME OBSERVATIONS

The following observations are included for the interest of all fighter pilots and others associated with the business of aviation.

**Air vice-Marshal Abbas Mirza** made an observation after reading the above crash story of Alamdar. According to Mirza,

"I think you are mixing the word 'back-pressure.' Back pressure is a feeling in the hands when pulling back on the stick to initiate a climb or to enter into a high G turn. It should not be confused with holding the stick back to maintain or accelerate the turn or climb angle. Loss of back pressure to me does not make sense. Do you mean there was no response from the elevators? Then the situation would be where the stick becomes loose in the pilot's hands. Is that what happened? Secondly, the bump is ominous. It indicates a mid-air collision."

**Wing Commander Irfan Masum** in responding to AVM Abbas said,

"I value AVM Abbas' comment, as he is a veteran fighter pilot of note. However, I would like to explain the 'back pressure' issue further. During the manoeuvres, any time g's were to set in, the leader would call 'back pressure'. This would indicate to the rest of the formation members that g's were coming on so that they could anticipate what to do next. Otherwise they would be left out of position when the g's actually set in. After the g's came on, the leader would hold a set amount of back pressure on the stick (especially for the steep turn) to maintain the height. Whenever the slot man got too close under the leader's tail, it would disrupt the airflow from the elevators and the leader would sense a loss of back pressure with which he was holding the stick. It would actually reduce the g's. With no prior warning to the formation members (who would be holding the earlier set-in g's), they would suddenly be thrown above the leader's aircraft (referred to as a bump). In all probability the slot man would go and hit the leader's tail. This used to happen sometimes and we had figured out why. Therefore, as soon as the leader would sense the loss of stick back pressure, he would call out for the slot man to move back a little (without being able to see him). The two wing men could see the slot man's nose through their peripheral vision and knew exactly where he would affect the leader's loss of stick back pressure. Perhaps 'loss of back pressure' can be substituted with 'loss of stick back pressure' to avoid any confusion". Irfan used the word 'bump' for lack of a better word - it refers to being in position and then getting thrown above the lead aircraft in an instant.

**Air Commodore Pervaiz Akhter**, who mentioned the hardness of the skin in Alamdar's hands, responded by saying,

"When the low pressure of the canopy of the rear aircraft interacts with high pressure of the lower side of lead aircraft, the lead aircraft pilot had to apply more than the normal pressure...Back pressure to keep the aircraft in a tight turn. That is what caused the calloused hands of Alamdar. We don't know what exactly happened at the time of impact, but it meant loss of control."

*Alamdar*

*Shahid Nisar*

*Irfan Masum*

*Sherdil Formation*

# Crash of Flying Officer Hafeez

Flying Officer Hafeez was a No. 18 Squadron Pilot of F-86 single engine transonic high-speed jet fighter aircraft. Squadron Leader M.M. Alam, famous ace pilot of the Pakistan Air Force, had downed five Indian aircraft in less than a minute while flying the F-86 Saber jet aircraft.

Hafeez was a coursemate and Squadron Pilot of Flying Officer Adil Rasheed. Hafeez was my senior Flight Cadet at PAF academy, Risalpur. He had a quiet and smiling personality. He crashed because of structural failure of the F-86 in a formation of four aircraft led by Flight Lieutenant Shujaat Azeem. Flying Officer Adil was officially detailed by the Squadron Commander to inform Hafiz's family about the crash. Hafeez came from a humble family in Karachi where his father ran a small tailor shop. Adil told me that when he informed Hafiz's father about the crash, he gracefully stood up without a tear in his eye. He told his wife that her son had become a martyr in the line of duty. His mother on hearing the news cried, but his father kept the graceful posture of the father of a martyr.

# Exploded in the Air!

Flying Officer Sikander Shah became the first martyr of our 65th G.D.(P.) course when he crashed over the Jamrud firing range. The Saber F-86 aircraft he piloted exploded in midair while pulling up after firing at the target.

Flying Officer Najam Saeed, another coursemate of ours, flew as No. 3 in the same formation and witnessed the crash. He narrated the accident. After leading the prestigious 'Sherdil' formation of the T-37 aerobatic team at Risalpur Academy, Najam also served as an instructor pilot of F-16 aircraft. He earned four-star green endorsements for safe flying and efficiently handling emergencies.

Sikander Shah was a lively, handsome, likable, and intelligent officer of our course. Our cadetship days of Lower Topa and Risalpur were filled with our association of good and tough times. Later in 1978, we served together at Air Base Masroor as pilot officers. He belonged to No. 2 Squadron of T-33 aircraft while I was a part of the Air Traffic Control Squadron. He often responded with a smile at the naughty remarks of his coursemates. Sikander came from the family of renowned Indian actor Naseer-ud-din Shah and had a striking resemblance to him.

The fatal accident that took Sikander away from us occurred whilst he was flying in No. 26 Squadron during a ground attack phase at Peshawar Air Base. On that fateful morning, according to Najam they took off in a three-ship formation for the gunnery mission over the range. Squadron Leader Tariq Nasim, instructor pilot, was the leader. Sikander Shah was No. 2 and Najam followed as No. 3 in the formation. According to their preflight briefing on the ground, after takeoff they were to join in a close formation and set course for the Jamrud firing range. After joining in close formation they checked by radio with the Range Safety Officer (RSO) and carried out the spacer run - the first dry run over the firing range to create a desirable space between the aircraft. This is followed by firing with a dive over the target and pull-up to exit safely after releasing the weapons. They peeled off into a left-hand gunnery circuit pattern and, one after the other, hit at the target while maintaining a safe distance between their aircraft.

RSO was a former squadron pilot. His job was to ensure a safe range for the required exercise with targets marked and laid out properly. He controlled and cleared all the aircraft for the exercise and passed on firing scores to the participating pilots. He also recorded all the range activities.

The formation carried hot guns because it was a gunnery mission. The Saber F-86 aircraft had six M3 Browning machine guns of .50 caliber with each capable of carrying 300 rounds. About halfway through the mission, as Najam started to roll in for the attack,

Sikander ahead of him pulled up at the same time after firing his bullets. From the corner of his left eye, Najam saw a big bright flash to his left around the position where Sikander should have been with his plane.

He turned his head towards Sikiandar's aircraft, expecting to see him pulling out of a dive in a left-hand climbing turn in gunnery pattern. But the controls shivered in his hands and Najam saw a huge ball of fire - like an inferno or an airburst of a Napalm bomb. Not knowing what had happened, he frantically looked around to see the aircraft of Sikander. All he saw was that dropping ball of fire. There was neither an aircraft nor a parachute. He immediately called off the attack, pulled out of the target, radioed his leader, Squadron Leader Tariq, and told him what he had seen.

When Tariq asked the RSO on the radio, the RSO froze due to shock of seeing the crash and did not respond immediately. After some time, the RSO came to life and reported that Sikander had crashed. Najam inside the cockpit, overwhelmed with horrible thoughts, didn't want to think the worst. He continued looking around for a parachute that wasn't there.

Ordered by Squadron Leader Tariq, Najam joined in close formation and reported the crash position to the Peshawar Control Tower. They circled over the firing range and headed back to the base. Peshawar Control Tower took crash action and sent the search and rescue helicopter with a Flight Surgeon on board.

Najam, after reporting to all the commanders about the accident, stood alone outside the squadron building in Peshawar. He kept looking towards the initial reporting position in the false hope of seeing Sikander returning with his plane. That was not to happen.

According to the postmortem report, he suffered more than 100 internal bone fractures, but surprisingly, his main body remained intact. A typical smile was on his lips when we saw his body before the burial. He left us more than thirty-six years ago, but his ever smiling face comes to mind whenever we talk about him.

The Inquiry Board determined 'structural failure' of one of the wings as the reason for his crash. It happened because of airframe fatigue. When Sikander started his pull-out from the dive with 4 to 5 g's, a tremendous load was imposed on the plane and broke the wing. The broken wing hit the fuel tank, immediately lighting the fire that exploded the aircraft in the air. Najam saw that huge fireball. The explosion shocked the pilot, setting him unconscious. Because of low altitude, he hit the ground before taking any evasive action. No. 26 Squadron grounded its fleet of the F-86 aircraft after that fatal crash of Flying Officer Sikander Shah.

Najam registered a few strange observations in his association with Sikander. After graduation, the Pak number first allotted to Najam was later transferred to Sikander. (In the Air Force, the Pak number determines the seniority of a person.)

Najam believed that better guns installed on a particular tail number aircraft resulted in better firing scores. Sikander was flying that aircraft. If asked, Sikander would have switched the aircraft with Najam.

Despite having a strong desire to switch aircraft with Sikander, Najam struggled hard in his mind and avoided asking for the switch. He often wondered if the **Pak number** and the **tail number** of the aircraft played a role in the crash of Sikander.

Najam carried a feeling from that day onwards that all three members of Sikander's formation were destined to die in an air crash. On the 7th of September, 1980, an aerobatic practice show at Masroor Air Base led to the crash of Squadron Leader Tariq (Leader of Sikander's formation). He embraced martyrdom performing an aileron roll over the base, and Najam witnessed a crash once again - this time from the ground.

Najam considers himself destined to have witnessed the air crash of two comrades. Najam retired as a Wing Commander from service and now lives in Toronto.

*Standing from Left: Sikander Shah, Ayub Chaudhry, Aziz-Ullah-Qazi
& Asif Aziz Shah*
*Sitting from Left: Abdul Rehman, Pervez Tabassum, Tubrez Asif
& Najam Saeed Qureshi*

# Crash of my Roommate - Asif Aziz Shah

The late Flight Lieutenant Asif Aziz Shah and Air Commodore
Amjad Bashir, as Flight Cadets, were my barrack mates in Lower
Topa and roommates in Risalpur. Asif shifted to the Under-
Officers block after becoming the Wing Under Officer - the highest
appointment held by a cadet. All three of us came from the city
of Rawalpindi. After joining the Air Force, we came to know one
another and formed an instant bond of friendship.

Asif had an elder sister Nilo and was an only son. Uncle Shah, his
father, was a Pathan, and his mother came from a refined Urdu-
speaking family. Both parents were kind and friendly toward us.
Uncle Shah was popular among us, as he would joke liberally and
treated us like friends. We visited Uncle Shah even when Asif was

147

not at home. Asif's mother always treated us like her children and served us lavish food.

We agreed that Asif was the most handsome and good-looking flight cadet on the course. Equally talented, he graduated with the Sword of Honour and the Best Pilot Trophy from the Academy in Risalpur. He later got posted to No. 18 Squadron of F-86s in Masroor, Karachi.

Asif was a talented fighter pilot with enormous potential to reach the highest position in the Air Force. He once discussed with me the possibility of quitting the Air Force. He wanted to provide a better lifestyle for his parents who had struggled hard in raising him. This was not possible with the limited salary of the Air Force. I reminded him of his potential success within the Air Force. He was well aware of his talent but left the Air Force for a better life for his parents. He started by joining the Flying Club in Karachi to earn a Commercial Pilot License (CPL) needed for joining the National Air Carrier that richly paid its pilots.

One morning in March, 1983 I received a call from his sister Nilo Aapa. She was crying and between her sobs she told me that Asif was no more in this world. The news was shocking. After recovering from the first shock of the devastating news, I told my wife to get ready, and we immediately rushed to his home in Defence Society of Karachi. There lay his dead body dressed in white, all clean in a single piece with a smile on his face - unlike most air crash victims.

Asif's wife Nasira sat there with tearful swollen eyes. Unable to speak, she silently looked at the dead body of her husband. Her young daughter Nageen ran around without knowing why so many people were crowded in her house. The parents of Asif sat in complete shock with lots of pain on their faces. Nilo Aapa, Asif's elder sister, cried with tears rolling down her face. It was a sad place where everyone cried for the untimely death of a young, handsome pilot.

That day Asif had gone airborne with ex-Flying Officer Mushahid, who had earlier served as our instructor on the T-37 aircraft in Risalpur Academy. Mushahid had also left the Air Force and was completing his hours for the Commercial Pilot's License (CPL). Mushahid, for his confident handling of the controls, was considered a hot-rod pilot by his students.

The two were on a Banner-Tow mission in a Cessna-172 aircraft that, on her tail, had the advertising banner of a cold drink company. A tow mission carried a flag attached to the tail of the plane using a steel string. The flag attracted the attention of the public when flown over the city at a low height.

During their flight over the city, they made a fly-pass over Asif's home in Defence Society. He waved to his parents, wife, and two-year-old daughter, Nageen, who waved back to her Papa from the roof of her home.

After completing the mission, they released the banner from less than a hundred feet above the ground. Witnesses on the ground later revealed that they had pulled straight up after dropping the flag. Yet the aircraft immediately came back down after a vertical climb of a few seconds. Both the bodies were found intact, but they died instantly on impact with the ground.

Fighter pilots are trained to pull up hard because of the powerful jet engines that provide the thrust. The piston engine Cessna-172 was unable to sustain the hard pressure and stalled. Since there wasn't enough height to recover, the aircraft hit the ground and both pilots were killed. With Asif was buried the dream of providing a better life for his family.

It is important to mention what happened to the parents after the death of Asif. During the thirty-five years that they lived after his death, they were looked after by our coursemates.

The responsibility of their care was taken up by Shabbir Latif, who was with us from the 12th Pre-Engineering course of the Air Force.

Uncle Shah told me that whenever he was hospitalized, Shabbir always installed his bed on the hospital floor next to him and spent the night. This care continued until his death.

Some coursemates of Asif including Squadron Leader Maula, Colonel Afzaal Niaz, Squadron Leader Aziz-ullah-Qazi, and others regularly visited Uncle Shah and Auntie whenever they were in Karachi. On one of my visits from Canada to Karachi, I went to see Auntie in the hospital. She was in the bed with tubes attached all over her body. I said Salam to her and introduced myself, but she didn't respond as she was unconscious and unable to speak. The wife of Squadron Leader Yawar, a doctor by profession, stood there by her side. Shabbir Latif, Squadron Leader Qazi, Squadron Leader Saqib Khawaja, and Squadron Leader Yawar sat outside the room chatting with Uncle Shah. About an hour later, before leaving from the hospital, I again visited Auntie inside her room. This time, I whispered my name in her ear and offered my Salam to her. Unconscious, unable to speak, her eyes closed, a sweet smile confirming my Salam appeared on her face - she died a few months after my visit. Uncle Shah later revealed that upon recovery from unconsciousness she had enquired if I had visited her.

Air vice-Marshal Tubrez and his wife took great care of Uncle and Auntie. They visited them regularly with their children. It brought a smile to their faces when Tubraiz's children called them Daada and Daadi and behaved like their grandchildren. Tubrez brought them to his home often. This same routine was followed by Squadron Leader Azizullah Qazi and his family.

A month before his death, I received a call from Uncle Shah from Karachi. He sounded weak but spoke in his usual jolly style. Shabbir had organized the call. In fact, he called many other friends of Asif. What an irony of fate - Asif gave his life after making a move to another organization to provide a better life for his parents. He did not know that he had already secured their future by leaving his own loving and lasting impression on the company of his coursemates. Our course richly preserved the tradition of a proud comradeship.

When I contacted Asif's wife, bhabi Nasira, she spoke courageously about him. She loved him more than life. They were friends first and husband and wife later. Her life after the death of Asif was tough as she restricted herself to graveyard and home. Their married life had lasted only two years. She remembers that before his death, Asif had wanted her to be independent as he had planned on going abroad in search of a job. He would scream at her to learn how to drive - which she did before his death. It was because of the driving that she was able to keep her job and stay independent.

Asif loved his daughter to the extreme. Nageen learned everything about Asif through her mother. The pretty lady bhabi Nasira never married again. She spent her youthful years raising her daughter and staying connected to the memories of her loving husband. She calls her life with Asif a sweet dream - a dream that didn't last for long. Bhabi Nasira now lives in Dubai with her daughter and grandchildren.

*Nusrat with Asif on the day of his marriage*

*Asif receiving best pilot trophy from Air Chief Marshal Zulfiqar*

# "Standby" - The Last Words of Rizvi

Wing Commander Ejaz-Ud-din commanded No. 17 Squadron at the Masroor Air Base. It was comprised of the Chinese F-6 aircraft, also known as the Mig-19 - a twin-engine supersonic jet fighter with maximum speed of Mach 1.4. The Pakistan Air Force, after acquiring the aircraft from China, upgraded it by installing many different types of equipment designed to increase the overall ability of the aircraft. The major modification included the Martin Baker ejection seat, under wing tanks, and underbelly Gondola fuel tank. Modifications completed by the Pakistan Air Force ensured the safety of the pilot and increased the fuel endurance. The AIM-9 Sidewinder air-to-air missile and French 68mm rockets provided a better weaponry system. Engineers of the PAF also designed a special Auxiliary Power Unit (APU) for instantly starting its twin engines and thereby decreasing the scramble time.

Flight Lieutenant Hasan Haider Rizvi was a tall, handsome, fair-coloured, smart young pilot of the No. 17 squadron. He graduated from the famous Cadet College Petaro of Hyderabad and joined the Air Force with the 59th G.D.(P.) course. He held the highest appointment of Wing Under Officer during cadetship at the Lower Topa Air Base and was awarded the Sword of Honour upon graduation from the Risalpur Academy. I had known Rizvi for about a year after my first posting to Air Base Masroor. We played cricket together in the Base team and often met in the daily ATC morning briefings conducted in the Wing briefing room. Rizvi was a witty person, always smiling or telling interesting anecdotes in the company of his junior or senior officers. He loved flying and grabbed every opportunity to get airborne.

On the 15th of August, 1979, Flying Officer Imtiaz from 64th G.D.(P.) course was sitting in the Squadron tea bar when Flight Lieutenant Rizvi asked him to perform the duty of Mobile Officer. Imtiaz had also studied at Petaro Cadet College and was a couple of years' junior to Rizvi. They were now squadron pilots of No. 17 squadron and enjoyed healthy comrade relations. Rizvi wanted to fly a

Functional Check Flight (FCF) mission in an F-6 aircraft cleared by the maintenance squadron. There wasn't any urgent requirement to fly that afternoon. Some squadron pilots had even asked Rizvi to fly the next day, but his love of flying - or the prescribed time of death - took him to the cockpit on that ill-fated day.

Imtiaz dropped Rizvi at the tarmac and soon settled at the mobile for runway 27. Rizvi "Tiger-105" taxied out and took off normally on that sunny afternoon. The only other F-86 aircraft in the air landed soon after Rizvi had taken off. As there were no other aircraft in the air, Tiger-105 was cleared by the Air Traffic Control Tower to operate overhead the air field from 10,000 feet to 30,000 feet. After the mission Rizvi asked for joining instructions. Tower cleared him to join for Runway 27. When Tiger-105 did not report his position at joining point, the Control Tower called him after about five minutes and asked,

"Tiger-105 Masroor Tower, request your estimates for Qilla (joining point)."

Tiger-105 responded by saying "Standby." Another five minutes passed, yet Tiger-105 didn't respond. Therefore, Control Tower again asked his position. He again responded by saying "Standby." When Control Tower called him for the third time, he sharply responded, "Standby." Flying Officer Imtiaz thought that the response sounded somewhat annoyed as if he were battling some emergency and didn't like to be disturbed. A long pause prevailed and Tiger-105 didn't call back. Control Tower called him many times and the Mobile Officer also called to find out his position, but silence prevailed. There wasn't any response from Tiger-105. Control Tower and Flying Officer Imtiaz then saw some smoke rising north of the airfield.

Flight Lieutenant Waris and Flying Officer Sheharyar were pilots of the Search and Rescue Helicopter Squadron. They spotted the wreckage a few miles to the north of the airfield away from the downwind position of the Masroor circuit. From the cockpit of the rescue chopper, they saw that the drop tanks were scattered around the burning fuselage without any sign of a blossomed parachute or a pilot waving from the ground. After putting down the helicopter they saw some parts of the body spread around the aircraft. Shehayar recovered the bloodstained identity card of Flight Lieutenant Rizvi from the debris. The medical crew and the Flight Surgeon on board the chopper collected pieces of the human body and brought it back to the base. As such, "Standby" remains the last word of Flight Lieutenant Rizvi. He was unmarried and lived with his parents in the city of Karachi. He was buried with the Air Force contingent offering proper respect.

According to Flying Officer Imtiaz, that particular F-6 aircraft had been reported for fumes in the cockpit a few times before. The exact cause of the crash could not be ascertained, but most likely the pilot had become intoxicated by breathing in fumes. This may have been a factor in his crash. Waris lives in Pakistan; Sheharyar now lives in Canada. Imtiaz is now a captain on the Airbus.

# S.T. Eject, you are on Fire!

Sohail Tanveer Chaudhry, popularly known as S.T. in the Air Force, was a pilot of the No. 18 squadron of F-86 aircraft on my first reporting to Air Base Masroor. S.T. was a few courses senior to me. We became close while playing together for the Base cricket team. We also played billiards and table tennis. S.T. would often win in table tennis, but in billiards we remained an even match. Our friendship grew further. Consequently, I stopped calling him Sir and started addressing him as S.T. I enjoyed this privilege with two seniors, Pir Adil being the other.

Once, one of S.T.'s coursemates became angry with me for calling S.T. by his first name without using the word Sir. S.T. gave a big laugh and told him not to worry. Because of our strong friendship, S.T. also became a signatory on my marriage papers. Later, our families became close, and we often visited each other.

In the year 1993 while serving the Bahrain Air Force I came to know about the crash of S.T.Chauhdry. I contacted several course-mates of S.T. in the Pakistan Air Force to find out about the details of his crash. He crashed in Abu Dhabi while on deputation with the Abu Dhabi Air Force. Therefore, details of his crash were unknown to most officers in the Pakistan Air Force. Usman Sohail, eldest son of S.T., was twelve years old when his father crashed. He joined the Pakistan Air Force and eventually became a Squadron Leader and a pilot of JF-17 Thunder aircraft. Air Marshal Farhat Hussain, another coursemate of S.T., provided me with information about how to contact both Usman and Squadron Leader Mohammed Sultan, leader of the formation when S.T. crashed.

Consequently, I contacted them both by phone. Usman was overjoyed to receive a call from his father's friend. While talking about S.T. both of us became overwhelmed. We cried and then disconnected the phone. After some time, I again called Usman and together we cherished some fond memories of his childhood and our happy times with his parents.

Squadron Leader Sultan recognized me at once when I contacted him twenty-three years after the crash. He was the leader of the two ship mirage formation and the last man in contact with S.T. before he embraced martyrdom. Squadron Leader Sultan provided me with details of the crash. Wing Commander Amjad Rathore, another coursemate of S.T. and a mutual friend, also served the Abu Dhabi Air Force. Families of S.T. and Rathore were close - they got together on a weekly basis.

According to Rathore, on the day before the crash he received a late night call from S.T. who insisted that he come and visit his home at that time. With the next day being a workday, Rathore tried to avoid the visit. It was already past 10 pm, his children were asleep, and S.T. lived a forty-five-minute drive away from his home. Upon hearing his negative response, S.T. asked him to give the phone to Bhabi, wife of Rathore. S.T. then pleaded with her to visit. As a result, Rathore finally agreed.

Rathore put their sleeping children in the car and drove to S.T.'s home. They drank tea and enjoyed a friendly chat. They left at midnight. After the crash, Rathore noted that S.T. did not mention anything special that night. He just wanted to see his pal. Knowing S.T. well, I am aware of his friendly habits.

According to Squadron Leader Sultan, they were on deputation with the Abu Dhabi Air Force. On that fateful day of August 31st, 1993, they entered the cockpit to fly a low level navigation mission of three mirage aircraft. Captain Muabarak of the Abu Dhabi Air Force was the Leader, S.T. was No. 2, and Sultan was No. 3 in the formation. Sultan did not observe anything abnormal on the ground, and the briefing and taxiing out went smoothly as planned.

At take-off point the leader of the formation, Captain Mubarak, aborted due to technical reasons. As per the standard practice and briefing on the ground, Sultan from the No. 3 position took over as leader of the formation that had been reduced to two mirage aircraft.

They took off and flew over different islands according to their planned navigational route. On the final leg, while in battle formation, S.T. was about a mile away right abeam Sultan in visual contact, but a little low.

Sultan heard a garbled and noisy transmission in his headset and radioed, "Confirm No. 2 calling." He again heard same garbled noisy transmission. He was unable to understand anything, yet he was sure that the transmission originated from his No. 2.

"S.T., let us climb a little to have better R/T," Sultan transmitted and then he climbed. Hearing no response, he started turning right towards the aircraft of S.T.

He was still away closing in when Sultan witnessed S.T.'s aircraft on fire and bouncing over the water. He immediately called, "No.

2, eject, you are on fire." Hearing no response, he repeated his call two or three more times: "S.T., eject, you are on fire."

The aircraft bounced twice on the water in level flight. Although the fire disappeared every time the aircraft hit the water, the fire reappeared as soon as the aircraft emerged out of the water. The third time the aircraft bounced in a nose dive position and did not resurface.

Despite repeated ejection calls given by Sultan, nothing ejected out of the aircraft. He arrived overhead of the accident area and found nothing except water all around. He gave a "May-Day" call to the ATC and the radar. He kept orbiting over the crash site until reaching Texiico - the condition of low fuel.

Shaken by the loss of a comrade and friend, Sultan headed back and landed with tears in his eyes. The dead body of S.T. was later recovered intact, floating in the sea.

*Sqn. Ldr. S.T. Chaudhry*

*Sqn. Ldr. Usman Sohail- son of S.T. Chaudhry*

# Shakespearean Tragedy

## *CRASH OF A FATHER AND A SON*

Farida and Tariq were happily living in the officers' mess of the Air Force Base Masroor when on the sad afternoon of August 20th, 1980 the news arrived of her husband's crash. Married to Squadron Leader Tariq Nasim, she was happy and proud to be the wife of a fighter pilot of the Pakistan Air Force. She was working in the kitchen while her two children, a son and a daughter, were sleeping in the bedroom. Squadron Leader Tariq was also the leader of the earlier narrated accident that lost Flying Officer Sikander Shah over Jamrud Firing Range in Peshawer. F-86-F (American version of engine) aircraft of No. 26 squadron were grounded after the fatal crash of Sikander. Squadron Leader Tariq was later posted to No. 18 Squadron of F-86 E (Canadian version of engine) at Air Base Masroor. During the rehearsal of Air Force Day parade of September 1980, Squadron Leader Tariq was scheduled as standby pilot for Wing Commander Shahbazi, Officer Commanding No.

18 squadron of Sabers. At the last moment Shahbazi became engaged in another official duty. Squadron Leader Tariq, according to schedule, took over the mission.

Then Flight Lieutenant Raza, Pilot Officer Majeed, and SATCO late Group Captain Pir Naseer were present in the Control Tower of Air Base Masroor. Raza from the Control Tower remembered Tariq holding his position shortly after asking for taxi permission. He had reported a shimmy damper problem with the nose wheel of his aircraft. After fixing the problem he had gotten airborne from runway 27. According to Raza, the aircraft performed a wingover and made a low pass over the runway from 09 to 27. After that he made another wingover to reposition for an aileron roll while keeping the ATC tower as reference point. Raza remembered commenting on the flawed dipping nose of the aircraft during the roll, although this was soon adjusted. After crossing overhead the tower, Raza heard an 'OH' word from SATCO Naseer and turned back to see the folding wing flying away with the aircraft nose diving and hitting the hanger. Because of the low level there was no chance for ejection.

Everyday emergencies encountered by F-86 aircraft disturbed Group Captain Aman-Ullah, OC Flying Air Base Masroor at that time. He called Air Commodore Akber, Director of Flight Safety at the Air Headquarters, and briefed him about the deteriorating condition of the F-86s. Akbar tried to persuade AVM Bukhari (then ACAS Flight Safety) to ground the fleet of No. 18 squadron aircraft. Air Chief Marshal Anwer Shamim was then visiting America and a decision to ground the fleet of F-86s had to be taken on his return. F-86s of No. 18 squadron were grounded after the crash of Squadron Leader Tariq.

Farida, wife of Squadron Leader Tariq, was offered a teaching job at the Sargodha Air Force School and she was provided with accommodation in the officers' mess. Her son Imran Tariq followed the footsteps of his father by joining the Pakistan Air Force and graduating as a fighter pilot.

On the morning of April 8th, 2004, while preparing breakfast, Farida watched on television the news of a crash in Mianwali. Her heart sank after watching the news. Flight Lieutenant Imran, her son, was posted at Air Base Mianwali flying the F-7 aircraft. Later it was confirmed that the crashed plane had been flown by her son Flight Lieutenant Imran Tariq. Twenty-four years after the crash of her husband she was once again hit by the worst tragedy of her life. Her husband and son gave their lives serving the Pakistan Air Force.

Imran had performed Hajj few months before his crash. I didn't have the words to ask questions from a lady who had given her husband to her country when she was young and who had later lost her son when she was at the threshold of her old age.

Despite my many efforts, I wasn't able to extract any details of the crash of Flight Lieutenant Imran Tariq. I can only mention with certainty that Flight Lieutenant Imran Tariq crashed in an F-7 aircraft at Mianwali Air Base.

*Flt. Lt. Imran Tariq*

*Sqn. Ldr. Tariq Nasim*

# Major Babar (S.J.) - Downed by a Missile!

In the year 1984, after the ATC course from CATI Hyderabad, I was posted as the Senior Air Traffic Control Officer (SATCO) at the Pakistan Army Qasim Aviation Base of Dhamial. The base was about a forty-five-minute drive from my home in Islamabad. The base housed small aircraft and helicopters of the Pakistan Army. The Pakistan Air Force exercised command over the Control Tower. Other well-trained ranks of the Air Force controlled the Air Traffic. Then a Flight Lieutenant and a SATCO, I looked after the overall administrative and operational affairs of the ATC squadron.

Babar Ramzan was my schoolboy buddy from the same class of Central Government Model School in Satellite Town Rawalpindi. Because of our joint friendly extracurricular actions, Babar and I failed together in the same ninth class of the Central Government Model School in Rawalpindi. He led our naughty actions and I mostly followed him like an obedient student. After failing in the ninth class, he transferred to another school and was admitted in the tenth class without wasting a year. I, being a loyalist of Model School, stayed in the same class to repeat the lessons of the previous year.

During my posting as Senior Air Traffic Control Officer (SATCO) at Army's Qasim Aviation Air Base Dhamial, Captain Babar Ramzan performed as a helicopter pilot from the same Air Base. He lived a ten-minute drive from my home in Islamabad. Sometimes we carpooled. Captain Ateeq Malik, who also lived in the vicinity, was another helicopter pilot at the Base who joined us. Three of us in our respective Army and Air Force uniforms often carpooled together. On the way to the base and back home again we discussed all the good, the bad, and the ugly prevailing issues on the planet. We always remained in friendly contact. Ateeq retired after reaching the rank of full Colonel in the Pakistan Army.

On a chilly afternoon in August, 1992 Major Babar Ramzan, along with Major Khalid Sohail Sultan and Brigadier Masood Naveed, got airborne in a helicopter from the highest elevation battlefield of the Siachin area. They were carrying out reconnaissance on a Lama helicopter. The copter was hit by a missile fired by the Indian Army, killing all its occupants. Major Babar Ramzan and both of the other officers embraced martyrdom and were awarded the Sitara-e-Jurat, which is the third highest gallantry military award of Pakistan.

Babar loved the army more than his life. He gave his life in the line of duty while in uniform. Our mutual friend then Major Ateeq received the body of Babar in the Combined Military Hospital of Rawalpindi. He told me that Babar's body was intact and in one piece. Babar was in his flying overalls with a two-day beard and a smile on his face. Ateeq told me of touching Babar's face. Two days after his martyrdom it was soft and his overall was wet with fresh blood. Remembering Babar is like a walk down the memory lane of our younger years.

Babar left behind a wife and three children. His wife was a doctor; we had visited each other's families and shared some good times.

Unfortunately the younger son of Babar died in a road accident in New York.

During the sixties and seventies, Central Government Model School was one of the leading schools of Rawalpindi. One of the few co-educational schools of our time, Model School produced many notable citizens of Pakistan. The late Major General Ehtesham Zameer and Imtinan Zameer, sons of famous poet Major Zameer Jafri, came from this same school. Imtinan played first class cricket in Pakistan. Our class of about 25 students including the girls produced a few Generals of the Pakistan army. Brigadier Fiaz Satti, Brigadier Hafeez-uddin, and Major General Ahmed Bilal belonged to my class. Afia Mateen, our classmate who later moved to Bangladesh, married the person who rose to the rank of Major General in the Bangladesh army. Amin Hashim, Mazhar Billa, and Aziz Ansari retired as Lieutenant Colonels of the Pakistan army. The late Nadeem Kausar and Babar Ramzan reached the rank of Major in the Pakistan army. Irfan Malik, Khalid Iqbal, Sharaft Abbas, and Abrar Ahmed are prominent business people of Pakistan.

After failing in ninth class, I became a student of another class that mostly produced doctors. Dr. Nayyer Qazi, Dr. Saeed Alam, Dr. Maqbool Cheema, and Dr. Tahir Aziz were produced out of a class of 25 students. I and Wamiq Waheed Butt joined the Pakistan Air Force. Major Shahid Mehmood and Colonel Jawad joined the army. Mohsin Raza of our class is the captain of a Boeing 777 aircraft. Tahir Ikram and Mahmood Jilani made names serving the private sector. Zahid Naeem joined the civil services and Khizar Hayat became an engineer. Raja Idrees Akram enjoys a feudal life in Burewala. It is remarkable that most of us have maintained contact even today. We cherish our friendship of over fifty years.

Sirs Iqbal, Mahmood, Kiani, and Shah were some of the dedicated and talented teachers who, besides their respective subjects, taught us the meaning of life. Madams Naqvi and Surraya were efficient teachers who commanded our respect and love.

*From left: Saifi, Bilal, Baber Shaheed S.J.
Qazi, Ameen and Nusrat at the back*

*Children of Baber holding his Sitara-e-Jurrat and children of Nusrat*

# Chapter Ten
## *Democracy and Martial Law 1977-1988*

During my cadetship days from 1975 to 1977, Pakistan was passing through a period of democracy headed by Mr. Zulfiqar Ali Bhutto, the chairperson of the Pakistan People's party. Bhutto's biggest contribution to politics came through his initiative of addressing the basic needs of the poor. His slogan of 'Roti, Kapra, and Makan' (Food, Clothing, and Shelter) gained instant popularity with the poor and provided much needed confidence to the underprivileged public of Pakistan. In the history of Pakistan Bhutto will always be remembered for giving words to the voice of a people who remained under suppression during the earlier military rules of General Yahya Khan and Field Martial Ayub Khan.

Bhutto strengthened his position with absolute power through the voters. His political opponents, referring to his political victimization through the Federal Security Force (FSF) and the torture cells established at Dalai Camp, called him a dictator ruling under the blanket of democracy. Bhutto won the elections of March 1977, but all the opposition parties formed the Pakistan National Alliance (PNA) and accused him of rigging the elections. This conflict created huge unrest in the country.

General Zia-ul-Haq, then army chief of Pakistan, introduced martial law on the 5th of July, 1977 and promised to hold a fair election within 90 days. People distributed sweets on the streets to welcome the army. However, General Zia's conference with the political leaders later led to the banning of the political parties. Many political leaders were declared ineligible.

Under the regime of Zia-ul-Haq, Zulfiqar Ali Bhutto faced the death sentence by the Supreme Court of Pakistan on the charges of the murder of the father of Ahmed Raza Khan Kasuri, one of his political opponents. A split decision of the Supreme Court of Pakistan hanged Bhutto on the 5th of April, 1979. Hanging Bhutto was considered a judicial murder and questions were raised on the independence of judiciary in Pakistan.

Zia-ul-Haq introduced some stability to the country's economic growth and strengthened internal security. He introduced Islamic laws in the country. Clergy, for the first time in Pakistan, gained support of the establishment for an active role in the government. Introduction of the Shura Council (Islamic cabinet) and the Sharia courts initiated the Islamic system of justice in the country. Culprits found guilty of major crimes were flogged in public.

In 1979 the Russians invaded Afghanistan. Zia, on behest of the United States, became involved in the war that lasted over nine years from December 1979 to February 1989. It cannot be denied that Russian defeat in Afghanistan was not possible without the active participation of Zia through the ISI (Inter Services Intelligence - the master spy agency of Pakistan). The Afghan War also contributed to free trade of weapons and drugs into Pakistan from the porous borders of Afghanistan.

The promotion of clergy into politics created an influx of 'Madrassas' (religious Islamic schools). These 'Madrassas' were established in collaboration with the American Intelligence Agency, the CIA, and the Pakistani ISI. They produced thousands of Muslim freedom fighters from all over the world to fight against the invading infidel Soviet Union. Moscow finally withdrew in the beginning of 1989 from Afghanistan after costing millions of lives and billions of dollars.

Two weeks before the Russian withdrawal, on the 29th of January, 1989, the United States announced the closure of her embassy in Afghanistan. The Soviets and the Americans left behind a war-torn shattered Afghanistan that was soon occupied by the Taliban, an Islamic fundamentalist group comprised of the freedom fighters that were originally created and promoted by the CIA and the ISI to fight against the Russian forces. Osama Bin Laden later seized control of the group and launched worldwide terrorist operations. Zia-ul-Haq stayed in power until his death in an air crash in 1988. As such, his promise of returning to barracks after ninety days was extended to a little over eleven years of his rule.

# The Ohjri Camp Blast

Ohjri Camp was an ammunition depot of the Pakistan Army controlled by the Inter-Services Intelligence (ISI) located close to Faizabad on the Murree Road of Rawalpindi. Such a blast had never been heard before in the twin cities of Rawalpindi-Islamabad. The boundary wall of the Ohjri camp was also visible from the double road passing by the Rawalpindi Cricket stadium. On the 10th of April, 1988, about fifteen minutes prior to the blast, I passed through the same double road after performing night duty at Air Traffic Control tower Chaklala. I was on my way to my home in the G-9/3 sector of Islamabad. The blast occurred as I sat casually at the dining table and waited for my wife to prepare breakfast. The first blast was of a big magnitude, and it shook the earth below my feet. Still in my Air Force uniform of a Flight Lieutenant, I ran outside the home and noticed a huge black mushroom cloud of smoke rising in the sky from the direction of Rawalpindi.

The blast was followed by a whistling noise of flying missiles and projectiles falling in all directions. Some of these projectiles fell on the Margalla hills of Islamabad and lit small fires at many spots in the surrounding mountains. We later came to know the explosion had killed more than a hundred and injured over a thousand people. Mr. Khaqan Abbasi, a retired Air Commodore of the Air Force and then a federal minister, was killed when a missile hit his car. His son, who was also travelling with him in the car, remained in a coma for seventeen years before leaving for the eternal abode.

The blast had occurred at the ammunition depot of Ohjri camp. The depot included Stinger anti-aircraft missiles, antitank missiles, and long-range mortars. The President of Pakistan, General Zia-ul-Haq, at first called the explosion "an extraordinary accident", but later called it an act of sabotage.

A report by Michael Gordon published one week after the blast in *The New York Times* referred to Central Intelligence Agency (CIA) experts who believed in the possibility of this tragedy being an accident. However, the Defense department of the USA considered it an act of sabotage and pointed to a similar pattern of attacks against military setups by the agents of the Kabul regime. The State department of the USA termed it likely an accident or sabotage.

Some other contradictory comments about the blast appeared in the Pakistani press. One suggested the blast occurred when a truck bearing an Afghani license plate entered the compound and exploded. Another thought the blast might have been triggered when a Pakistani soldier dropped a white phosphorus shell in the storage filled with the Stinger anti-aircraft missiles.

Mr. Mohammed Khan Junejo, then prime minister of Pakistan, appointed two committees to investigate the debacle: a military committee formed under General Imranullah Khan, and a parliamentary committee headed by the veteran politician, Aslam Khattak.

Some unconfirmed reports stated that General Imranullah Khan held General Akhtar Abdul Rehamn responsible for the event. But General Zia-ul-Haq kept it under wraps, saving any harm to his relative and then Director General of the ISI. The investigation by Aslam Khattak did not blame anyone and declared it a sad accident.

Former Federal Minister Begum Kulsoom Saifullah, a veteran politician, published her Urdu book *Meri Tanha Pervaaz* meaning *My Solo Flight* released on September 14, 2011. She wrote in her book of starting work as a federal minister the same day the Ohjri Camp tragedy occurred. She believed some Stinger missiles taken from the depot were given to Iran. She was also convinced that General Zia-Ul-Haq had ordered the depot blown up to avoid the USA audit team due for inspection. However, her claims remained unfounded and did not make a serious impact at any reputable investigating agency. Different news sources reported that Iran had bought the Stinger missiles from the Afghan Mujahdeen. The USA audit team couldn't have discovered if there was a theft that Zia wanted to hide. He successfully hid from the Americans the presence of a nuclear bomb in Pakistan.

*Dawn*, a leading English daily newspaper of Pakistan reported in its publication of September 17, 2011, "Ms Safiullah started writing the book two years ago when she probably had not considered the possibility that those very same people who she labels "opportunists" would later end up as political aides for her sons."

According to *Dawn* her son Salim Saifullah said, "We are in trouble because I am president of the party and the book annoyed my secretary general Humayun Akhtar, son of General Akhtar Abdur Rehman." *Dawn* further reported that in order to control the damage, Saifullah's family tendered an apology and Mr Saifullah blamed the editor of the book instead of the author for what should not have been published in the autobiography. Mr Saifullah said, "We tendered our apologies not only to General Akhtar's family but also to others who have been hurt by Begum Kalsoom's revelations". The book lost credibility soon after its publication.

Many political analysts believed the government of Mohammed Khan Junejo was disbanded by Zia-ul-Haq because he insisted on making the report public. Interestingly, neither of the two investigation reports became public even later during the two civil regimes of Benazir Bhutto and Nawaz Sharif.

I was an Air Traffic Controller at Chaklala Air Base from 1984 to 1985 and from 1987 to 1988. During the late night hours we often received an American C-141 strategic Starlifter, a large jet designed to carry a huge amount of freight. Those flights always parked close to the Murree road end of the old secondary runway. A lengthy caravan of civil hired trucks lined up close to the aircraft and carried the ammunition off-loaded from the aircraft. The Pakistan Army strictly supervised the transfer and the trucks were dispatched one by one without drawing any concern or attention. The trucks offloaded their luggage into the well-guarded compound of the Ohjri Camp.

Continuous spraying of missiles from the dump stopped within a few hours of the first big blast. However, an occasional volcanic eruption of projectiles continued for the next few days. From Chaklala Tower I remember controlling a low-level mission of Mirage aircraft flown over the area of the blast. Infrared cameras fitted in the Mirage aircraft revealed the prevailing hot temperature below the ground. The Government of Pakistan contacted different companies in the United States and France for the cleanup operation. It had turned into a sleeping inferno because of the hot temperature in the underground storage of the depot. US and French experts demanded high payments and an estimated minimum period of six months.

General Zia-ul-Haq turned to Major General Javed Nasir from the Engineers Corps. He then headed the Joint Intelligence Technical (JIT), a department responsible for the counter-proliferation and promotion of science and technology in the military. General Javed was famous for being an honest religious man with his long white beard. He cleared the dump by setting a personal example of carrying the dangerous ammunition with his bare hands. The dump was cleared within fifteen days without a single casualty.

My high school classmate Bilal, then a Major in the Pakistan Army, served the ISI from his office inside the Ohjri camp. Twenty-eight years after the blast, at the time of writing this book, I called Bilal in Pakistan to refresh our memories about the blast and he spoke candidly to me. Bilal was attending Staff College at Quetta when the blast took place, but he believed it to be an act of sabotage conducted by someone with the help of an insider. The Americans had started buying back the Stinger missiles towards the end of the Russian occupation in Afghanistan. In Bilal's opinion some hostile intelligence agency which didn't want these weapons to be used by the Pakistan Army, nor by the Mujahedeen in the future, got the job done with the help of some faction of the Afghan Taliban. Bilal retired from the army after rising to the prestigious rank of Major General.

*Major General Bilal*

*Nusrat and Major General Ahmed Bilal*

# Pakistan ONE Crashed

The flight plan of 'Pakistan One' came in for my signature on the night of August 16th, 1988. I was the Duty Air Traffic Controller (DATCO) in the Control Tower at the Air Force Base Chaklala. Pakistan One had filed a return flight plan to and from Bhawalpur because the regular Air Traffic Control service was not available at the Bhawalpur airfield. It showed an early morning departure of a C-130 aircraft carrying Pakistan One, President of Pakistan General Zia-ul-Haq.

The flight plan identified Wing Commander Mashud as the captain and Flight Lieutenant Sajid as the copilot of the aircraft. I had personally known both the pilots - I played cricket in the Base cricket team captained by Wing Commander Mashud. He was a soft senior who maintained a friendly atmosphere during our cricket matches. Flight Lieutenant Sajid was a respectful junior who sometimes visited the Control Tower. Squadron Leader Zulfiqar, a sober and decent officer, acted as the navigator of that ill-fated plane. Squadron Leader Rahat, an instructor pilot from my cadetship days at Risalpur, had also boarded the plane as aide-de-camp (ADC) of General -Zia-ul-Haq. After performing night duty on my way home in the morning, I had to stop my jeep because of the red light on the barrier installed at the road connecting the tarmac of the VVIP aircraft. Because of the flight plan that I had signed late the previous night, I knew that the red stoplight was for the President of Pakistan who must be on his way to the aircraft. Soon the presidential motorcade passed in front of me. I saw General Zial-ul-Haq engaged in a conversation with General Akhtar Abdul Rehman who accompanied him in the back seat of the black limousine. That was the last time I had a personal glimpse of General Zia-ul-Haq and General Akhtar Abdul Rehman.

On the evening of August 17th, 1988, the crash of the C-130 carrying General Zia-ul-Haq hit the media headlines in Pakistan and all around the world. In addition to the ten top generals of the Pakistan Army, it also carried Arnold L. Raphel, the U.S. Ambassador and General Herbert M. Wassom, the U.S. Chief military attaché in Pakistan. Thirty-one people on board the plane died in that tragic crash. Brigadier Siddique Salik, a well-known literary personality of Pakistan, had also boarded that plane.

Many conspiracy theories erupted after the crash on the national and international screen. Within the country, some blamed the Shia community. A couple of weeks before the crash of General Zia, on the 5th of August, 1988, Allama Arif Hussaini, a renowned Shia leader and Chief of Tehrik-e-Jaffaria Pakistan (TJP), was murdered in Peshawar. Although General Zia attended the funeral of the slain leader, some from the Shia community blamed him for the murder of their leader. Flight Lieutenant Sajid, copilot of the crashed C-130, had recently converted to the Shia sect in religion and some thought that he had conducted a suicide mission to avenge the murder of Arif Hussaini.

**Flight Lieutenant Ramiz Gilani**, another C-130 pilot who had played a pivotal role in the conversion of copilot Sajid to the Shia sect, was taken in custody by the ISI (Inter-Services Intelligence). Later, he was released without a blemish. Claims of

Shia involvement remained unfounded. Ramiz rose to the rank of Air Commodore and retired after commanding the Chaklala Air Base.

**Ejaz-ul-Haq, son of General Zia**, in an interview on Geo TV, on December 1st, 2012, accused General Aslam Beg, then vice-Chief of the Army, of being the person behind the conspiracy to kill his father. He believed in the theory of a missile fired by another aircraft. Ejaz-ul-Haq further added that Beg had prevented autopsies of the dead to hide the facts; furthermore, Beg had ordered the removal of the plane wreckage. However, Ejaz-ul-Haq failed to provide any concrete evidence as proof for his claim.

Those who considered it an international conspiracy thought that Zia had created enmity with the Soviet Union by helping the Afghan Mujahedeen. His active role in the war made the Soviets face a humiliating defeat; therefore, K.G.B. involvement in the crash became an obvious logical choice. Other political analysts pointed towards the U.S. history of eliminating dictators after they had performed a wanted task. General Zia had outlived his role after the Russians had signed the withdrawal agreement. The USA lost interest in the region as well as in General Zia-ul-Haq. None of the international theories provided any concrete evidence associated with the crash.

**Air Commodore Shahid Kamal** acted as the Director of Operations/ACAS Plans for the Pakistan Air Force at Air Headquarters at the time. He claimed to be an instructor pilot of Mashud and a U.S. qualified Systems Safety Specialist trained by the USAF. His theory about the crash, which later floated onto Facebook, attracted some interest.

According to Kamal, "When an aircraft rotates during takeoff, the contents of the aircraft tend to shift rearward. Powerful steel and nylon restraints are used to prevent this from happening. If the restraints are slack, work loose, or break, then the contents will slide towards the tail of the aircraft. This will cause an attendant shift of the centre of gravity of the aircraft towards the rear. This rearward shift of the centre of gravity will cause the nose of the aircraft to pitch up. The pilot will note this pitch up and try to counter it by pushing forward on the stick." He termed this 'shift of the centre of gravity' to be the cause of the crash.

**Air Commodore Kazim**, my coursemate and a C-130 pilot, responded to the theory of Kamal. Kazim claims to have recreated the crash in a simulator. With the loss of elevator the aircraft behaved exactly the same way as it did at Bahawalpur. The only option to control the pitch emerged through power manual trim. It would overreact and bring aircraft into oscillation. Kazim believed that presence of some content of sulfur close to the elevator booster confirmed the theory that a small blast had ruptured the elevator control. Sulfur is a nonmetallic yellow element used to manufacture gunpowder.

**Air Commodore Abbas Mirza**, Assistant Chief of Air Staff Flight Safety, headed the Board of Inquiry formed by the Pakistan Air Force. The Board also included Air Commodore Muzamil Saeed, Group Captain Zaheer Zaidi, and Wing Commander Sabahat Ali Mufti. The Board was comprised of professional engineers, fighter pilots, and a C-130 pilot. Six Air Force technicians from the USA also assisted the board. The board visited the crash site and re-created the actual crash. It interviewed many eyewitnesses on the ground and thoroughly examined the wreckage. About forty key pieces of engines, fuel lines, pumps, fluid samples, and many other items of the destroyed aircraft were sent to U.S. and Pakistani laboratories for different analyses. The board sought expert advice from the Lockheed Company, makers of the C-130 Hercules plane. It also engaged many professionals from the fields of explosives, flame patterns, forensic analysis, aircraft instruments, and airframe structures.

After intensive scrutiny and investigation, the technical inquiry headed by Air Commodore Abbas Mirza submitted a report that spread over 350 pages. The report failed to find any technical reason or pilot error. It pointed to an act of highly sophisticated sabotage. There were no traces of a hit from the ground or air; however, some aircraft parts were found contaminated with strong traces of antimony, potassium, sulfur, phosphorus, and, most significantly, pentaerythritol tetra nitrate (PETN) - an explosive used in highly sophisticated sabotage operations. It is believed that shortly after takeoff the detonation of some poisonous gas in the cockpit instantly paralyzed and incapacitated the pilots without even giving them a chance to transmit any emergency call.

The autopsies on the bodies recovered from the crash could have provided some clues to the crash. The inquiring team did not find an intentional omission of autopsies. The condition of the bodies likely required immediate burial. The American team of FBI agents investigating the crash insisted that it was due to technical failure, but could not produce any solid evidence.

The C-130 Hercules aircraft was considered to be the safest aircraft available in the aviation fleet. According to the U.S. Air Force, until 1989 it had a wear and tear rate of five percent compared with ten percent for the B-52 bomber and twenty percent for other fighter aircraft. The PAF, which has been flying the C 130 since 1962, has flown hundreds of thousands of hours. It has not had an accident before or since the mishap of Pakistan One. Quite a coincidence!

American Ambassador Arnold L. Raphel had gone to Bhawalpur in another small twin engine aircraft. General Zia-ul-Haq had gone to witness the field demonstration of the M-1 tank which Pakistan was considering purchasing from the United States. After the demonstration he invited the U.S. ambassador to board with him on his C130. General Wassom, the U.S. chief military attaché, joined them in the presidential flight. The pilot of the aircraft with the call sign 'Spark-63' who brought the U.S. Ambassador and the chief military attaché to Bhawalpur took off for Islamabad without his passengers. Like many other assassinations of high profile personalities in the past, the identity of the people involved in the crime remains a mystery.

## FURTHER INFORMATION

Excerpt from *The Last Salute* regarding the crash was published in *The Miracle* and *The Muslim Journal,* local newspapers of Vancouver. Much interesting information was passed on to me by various people who somehow bore witness or became involved with different aspects surrounding the crash. I have decided to include all of the relevant information for the interest of my readers.

**Air Marshal Dilawar Hussain** at the time of the crash performed as Deputy Chief of the Air Staff (DCAS) for Operations (OPS). He wrote to me that his afternoon nap was disturbed by a telephone call from Air Officer Commanding (AOC) the Air Defence. AOC informed him about the crash of Pakistan One killed with all passengers on board. Vice-chief of the Army Staff, General Aslam Beg, was on his way to Dhamial Air Base in a separate aircraft after circling over the crash site. Chief of the Air Staff Air Chief Marshal (ACM) Hakimullah Durrani was not traceable. Dilawar thinks that although Hakimullah hadn't ever played golf before the crash, nor did he golf after the crash, he was reported to be at the Pindi Golf Course at the time of the crash. Air Commodore Bukhari was sent with a first generation mobile phone to locate the Air Chief at the Pindi Golf Course. Dilawar meanwhile rushed to the Central Operation Command (COC) where AOC monitored the in-air situation.

Air Marshal Dilawar wrote to me, "On that fateful day I did what I could do to put the country on constitutional path." When in contact with the Air Chief, Air Marshal Dilawar passed him the arrival time of General Aslam Beg and suggested that he pick up the Naval Chief, Admiral Mohammed Khan, and that he receive General Aslam Beg at the Dhamial Air Base of Army Aviation. Dilawar proposed that the Air Chief and the Naval Chief should not ask General Beg what to do; they should rather jointly suggest the constitutional solution as the best and the only option even before the General met any of his Army colleagues. According to the constitution, the Chairman of the Senate would become the President of Pakistan after the death of General Zia-ul-Haq.

The Air Chief, the Naval Chief, and General Aslam Beg were the three top men of Pakistan after the crash of General Zia-ul-Haq and they were to decide the fate of Pakistan that evening. They decided to follow the constitution. After consultation on the Dhamial base tarmac, they went straight to the house of the Chairman of the Senate, Mr. Ghulam Ishaq Khan.

When the three chiefs arrived at the residence of Ghulam Ishaq Khan in Islamabad, his loyal Pathan servant refused to wake up the chairman who was enjoying a sound sleep. It was because of the Pushtoo language used by the Air Chief that the Pathan servant finally woke him. Mr. Ghulam Ishaq Khan at first refused to take over as the President of Pakistan, but then agreed when the three top men assured that they would back him up.

In his emails to me, Air Marshal Dilawar commented on the investigation by mentioning that the chief of the U.S. investigation team did call on him twice or thrice to advance the theory of "technical failure". He said that a "Mule" was not available; therefore, the hydraulic systems were not checked that led to hydraulic system failure. Dilawar told them that a 'Mule' equivalent ground hydraulic pump of British origin was available and was used to check all hydraulic systems of the C-130 aircraft. Mule is the US nickname of the ground trolley hydraulic pump. It is used to check aircraft hydraulic systems on ground during maintenance and aircraft inspections.

According to Dilawar, the American heading the U.S. investigation team presented another theory that blamed the Indians for the sabotage. Additionally, if Indian involvement was revealed, it would lead to a war between India and Pakistan as the Indians had killed the President of Pakistan. Dilawar responded by saying that Pakistani law does not stipulate any such thing, but the U.S. law makes it compulsory for the U.S. government to take punitive action against the perpetrators involved in the killing of U.S.

citizens. He also told the U.S. General about the Gulf of Tonkin incident that initiated the Vietnam War. Dilawar then reminded him of the U.S. citizens killed in the crash: Ambassador Raphel and General Wassom, the chief military attaché in Pakistan.

Dilawar as the DCAS (Ops) was supposed to write his remarks on the inquiry, but he was not shown the inquiry report. The American heading the U.S. investigation team never returned to his office.

Air Marshal Dilawar concluded that there was plenty to speculate, but there was 'NONE' in the form of advance, proven, or concrete pure evidence. Air Marshal Dilawar thought that after another two years or so the American government would reveal certain facts surrounding the crash at the expiry of the thirty-year period to declassify the secret documents. When I persuaded him further to share his personal opinion on the crash, Air Marshal Dilawar backed off by saying that he would reveal further facts in the book that he intended to write one day.

**Major Sohail Iqbal,** popularly known as Scopee by his friends, was a commando of the Special Services Group (SSG). He had served the Commando battalion of the Pakistan Army during my tenure at the Cherat Approach Control. He was posted in Bhawalpur as an undercover intelligence officer at the time of the crash and had reached the site within few minutes after the crash. He talked to an eye witness immediately after the crash who had observed the behaviour of the aircraft from the time of takeoff until it hit the ground. Based on his interview with the witness, Sohail discards all the theories presented so far. He thinks that the aircraft had turned around for landing back at Bhawalpur due to some emergency. Sudden lifting of the aircraft on final approach was due to the presence of a low tension electric wire in the path of the aircraft. In his opinion there wasn't any explosion of significant nature in the aircraft. The presence of PETN reported in the forensic report was from the percussion cap filling in the bullets of the hand gun carried by Naib Subaidar Shafique who was on board as the gun man of General Zia. These bullets were recovered unfired and intact.

**Brigadier Sagheer,** Director Internal Wing (IW) of the ISI, during my tenure in the ISI in 1989, once mentioned to me, "The killers of Zia-Ul-Haq were hiding in the Air Force." About twenty-nine years after the crash, I managed to contact Brigadier Sagheer in Pakistan and I reminded him of his words regarding the crash. He remembered his words and claimed to be the only person knowing the actual reason and details surrounding the crash. He would present all the facts in the book that he was writing and did not return my telephone when I tried to ask further about the crash.

## *SECRET REPORT BY GROUP CAPTAIN ZAIDI*

Late Group Captain Zaidi, Ops Investigator of the Mishap Team, had prepared a secret report and sent it to some of his confidants. Another Air Force Officer and a student of Group Captain Zaidi had also received some portions of that secret report. After reading my article regarding the crash of *Pakistan One* published in the local community newspapers of Vancouver, a student of the late Zaidi who lives in Australia sent me a portion of the secret report that he had received from Zaidi. Below is a synopsis from the short report received by me.

Group Captain Zaidi, in his own words, claims to have surfaced the report fifteen years after the crash. He adds further,

"I informed the FBI at three different occasions about this mishap i.e., first time on March 18th, 1995 at US Consulate in Karachi – Pakistan; the second time on December 8th, 1998, at my son's residence in Springfield Virginia; and lastly on January 4th, 1999 at FBI Field Headquarters at 4th Street NW in Washington DC. FBI Special Agent Mr. Andre Khourie asked me six times during the course of my interview on the last occasion as to how I was still alive and why my life was spared by the U.S. Government."

According to Zaidi, he was the only qualified mishap investigation expert available in the Air Force at that point in time. On the 16th of August, 1988, a day before the crash of Pakistan One, he was personally ordered by the Vice Chief of Air Staff (VCAS) Air Marshal Farooq Feroz Khan to report to the Air Headquarters in Chaklala from Karachi where he was investigating the crash of a mirage aircraft that had taken the life of Flying Officer Khalid Saifullah, and twelve civilians on the ground. Zaidi had applied murder charges on the OC No. 35 Fighter Wing, OC No. 8 Tactical Attack Squadron (TA Sqn), Flight Commander No. 8 TA Squadron the Mirage Formation Leader, and the Combat Commander School PAF Instructor Pilot after determining that Flying Officer Khalid had lost his life due to their negligence.

When Air Marshal Farooq asked him the reason for applying murder charges, Zaidi writes,

"It was murder and that the pilot was not mission compatible. All the five senior supervisors and fighter pilots forgot to notice that Flying Officer Khalid Saifullah had never practiced a mass raid mission on an airfield. That he had a total flying experience of 265 hours, while seven PAF Squadron Leaders flying that Mass Raid mission with him had 2,500 flying hours."

Zaidi claims that he was ordered to report to the Air Headquarters in Chaklala on the pretext of placing murder charges to the Air Force Pilots. Zaidi thinks that in reality, the Air Force higher command was aware of the crash that occurred the next day and he being the only investigation expert was positioned to become a part of the cover up operation. Zaidi wrote that he had thwarted the 'Super Power' designs to cover up the murder of thirty-one people. According to him, "Mr. Robert Oakley wanted to make the PAF Base Chaklala's poor maintenance of the C-130 fleet as the most plausible cause of the crash, and creating a technical fault to match and corroborate the cause was never a problem in the table inquiry. The C-130 Crash was intended to be made an avoidable maintenance factor accident. Every possible effort was made by almost everyone (except me) to make it look like a mechanical failure accident."

Zaidi, after praising the leadership qualities and war tactics adopted by General Zia ul Haq during the Afghan War, writes:

"Late General Zia was against the signing of the Geneva Accord in May, 1988. He had instructed Mr. Zain Noorani, the then Foreign Minister of Pakistan, not to sign the Geneva Accord in its present form. During that period Mr. Zain Noorani received two telephonic messages in Geneva from Mr. George Shultz, the then U.S. Secretary of State, that he must sign the Geneva Accord as soon as possible. Mr. George Shultz had assured him that he would remain the Foreign Minister of Pakistan for as long as he lives. Mr. Zain Noorani was very sorry on his deathbed that he had betrayed Late General Zia on a false promise made by the U.S. Secretary of State."

Zaidi claims that General Mirza Aslam Beg had sent his whole family to USA about twelve days before the C-130 Crash and questions if that was a coincidence. He mentions further,

"General Zia was in the knowledge of the conspiracy hatched by General Mirza Aslam Beg, the Vice Chief of the Army Staff (VCOAS). General Zia had informed Mr. Sharif Uddin Pirzada on August 15th, 1988 that he was going to move against General Mirza Aslam Beg and his cronies on August 19th, 1988. However, General Zia did not know this fact that he was involved with the Americans in this conspiracy bid. But alas! Fate did not let that happen. General Mirza Aslam Beg and partners in murder got him two days earlier."

In his report Zaidi stated that Benazir Bhutto was a regular visitor at the residence of U.S. Ambassador in Pakistan, the late Mr. Arnold Lewis Raphael, and that she was planning and plotting all possible intrigues to get rid of General Zia through Central Intelligence Agency (CIA), RAW (Indian Intelligence Agency formed to plan dismemberment of Pakistan), and Al-Zulfiqar (her brother Mir

Murtaza Bhutto's controlled and sponsored terrorist organization, which is an off-shoot of PPP). Zaidi writes,

"The decision to remove him [General Zia] was taken by the U.S. President, Mr. Ronald Reagan, around mid-January, 1988. The Special Assistant to the President of United States and a Senior Director of the National Security Agency (NSA), Mr. Robert Bob Oakley, was tasked to plan the caper to murder General Zia. He made a failsafe foolproof plan, which, with the help of Pakistan Army (PA) and Pakistan Air Force (PAF) hierarchy, worked superbly. How could anyone suspect that PA [Pakistan Army] and PAF [Pakistan Air Force] higher ups were involved in murdering their own head of state and COAS? Mr. Oakley arrived as Ambassador Designate to Pakistan a day after the accident with complete U.S. presidential powers to control, contain, and cover up the investigation. Whatever proof of murder or sabotage that was provided had been due to all my efforts. The cloak and dagger secrecy prevailed throughout the investigation. Questioning of lots of material witnesses was not allowed. Despite all hurdles created, it is a factual mishap investigation story."

Zaidi died of a heart attack. However, the inconclusive report of Zaidi received by me did not offer any hard eveidence in support of his claims.

After my face to face, telephonic, and electronic conversations with Air vice-Marshal Abbas Mirza, Brigadier Sagheer Hussain, and Air Marshal Dilawar, I am convinced that they know more than what has been revealed so far. AVM Mirza did not wish to comment further than his report presented before the Parliament of Pakistan. Air Marshal Dilawar and Brigadier Sagheer softly brushed me aside by saying that they were in the process of writing a book, where they would disclose those facts.

In my research so far, I have tried to present the received facts with referred sources without any prejudice and by avoiding any personal opinion. I might write a book one day on the subject in detail. That book would carry my personal observations, opinions, and much more than what is narrated here.

Air Marshal Dilawar called it a splendid work of nature: "A man was placed to the highest position in Pakistan while he was sound asleep in his bedroom. As such Mr. Ghulam Ishaq Khan became the biggest beneficiary of the death of General Zia-ul-Haq."

# Release from the Service

Wearing my winter Blue Air Force uniform and shining black Oxford shoes, I adjusted the blue Air Force peaked cap on my head and winked in the mirror with a smile on my face. It was a cold day in February 1989 in Islamabad. Imagining I was Sean Connery as 007, I walked briskly to my white Mazda 1300. Then I drove to the Inter-Services Intelligence Headquarters, the famous ISI, for reporting on the first day of my duty as General Staff Officer-2 (GSO-II). Alas, my dream of meeting with the renowned General Hameed Gul, then Director General (DG) ISI in a long room with fascinating electronic gadgets, did not come true. The interview with the DG took place in an ordinary room. The DG considered it necessary to personally welcome every officer equivalent to and above the rank of Squadron Leader.

I headed a section comprised of Squadron Leader Iqbal Shafique (Navigator), Squadron Leader Javed (Pilot), and Flight Lieutenant Jameel from the Air Defence Weapon Corps. Two civilian intelligence officers and some other ranks of the Air Force performed other administrative duties. Squadron Leader Mazahar from the Air Defence Corps acted as GSO-I and Air Commodore Ghori performed as the Director.

After serving one year in the ISI, I considered leaving the service to explore the world outside Pakistan. When my wife agreed with my decision to quit the Air Force, I sought advice from a senior Air Force officer.

I had served as an Air Traffic Control Officer under Air Commodore Abbas Mirza when he was commanding the Rafiqui Air Base at Shore Kot. As an ATCO, one was always in direct contact with the highest authorities of the Base. With Air Commodore Mirza, I had also played cricket on Rafiqui's team. He was a good cricketer, a fine professional, and a great human being. He was then promoted to Air vice-Marshal serving as Air Officer Commander (AOC) North, stationed in Peshawar. I had always admired him.

I called and requested to meet with him for advice on a personal matter. He recognized me and granted a meeting in his office. The next day he carefully listened to my desire to leave the service. I will always remember the few lines that he asked me to write on my release application. He asked that I record the facts: "I joined the Pakistan Air Force on----this date, and got commissioned on ------this date. Due to personal reasons, may I please be released from the service under the existing rules and regulations?" AVM Mirza directed me to the appropriate wording of my application.

Over the next few weeks I kept thinking about initiating the application. I often discussed with Squadron Leader Iqbal my plan of leaving the service. One afternoon, after I had repeatedly talked about my plan, Iqbal sarcastically asked,

"Sir, why don't you apply in writing for release from the service?"

It was a valid question that made me think. Ten minutes after Iqbal left my room, I jotted down on paper the few lines given to me by AVM Mirza. I called in the administration clerk to type my release application.

When Squadron Leader Iqbal saw the small application, he laughed and said, "Sir, you don't mean to leave the service. You want to create an impression of leaving." Getting released from the service during those days was an uphill task. It required a story of compassionate arguments. My release application presented a non-serious impression. The release application, following the proper channels, was initiated and forwarded to GSO-I on the same day as the 'valid' question had been asked by Iqbal.

The application went to Squadron Leader Mazahir - GSO-I. He forwarded it to Air Commodore Ghori - Director. Ghori concurred with Mazahir and sent it to AVM Altaf Shah, then Deputy Director General ISI. From Shah the application went to the Director General ISI - Lieutenant General (R) Shams-ur-Rehman Kallu.

General Kallu had taken over command from General Hameed Gul after the crash of General Zia-ul-Haq when Benazir Bhutto became the Prime Minister. Kallu, amongst his troops, carried the sound reputation of a great general. He was the only DG ISI who commanded the formation as a retired Officer. Perception prevailed that Kallu liked Zulfiqar Ali Bhutto, the hanged Prime Minister of Pakistan and father of Benazir. Because of his liking for the hanged Bhutto, General Zia-ul-Haq ignored his promotion to the chair of Vice of the Army Staff. Benazir endorsed his deployment as the Director General of the ISI.

The ISI staff, in those days, consisted of personnel who were considered to be die-hard supporters of General Zia. With Aslam Beg as the Chief of Army Staff, the move of placing Kallu as the DG was thought to be an act of cleaning the ISI from the likes of General Zia.

After another few days of the move of my release application, I received a call from Squadron Leader Naeem Ghori, a friendly senior. He dealt with release applications of the officers at the Air Headquarters. He asked me to come to his office.

When I reached Air Headquarters he handed me the file of my release application. I noted the remarks of all the Air Force Officers who spoke strongly against my release from the service. However, I was surprised to observe the remarks of General Kallu. He had slashed the suggestion of all three of my senior Air Force officers and wrote, "The officer has applied for release which is duly recommended. Since the ISI is a sensitive place, the officer should be reverted to the Air Force."

I was pleased to see it. I knew that the Chief of Air Staff would not dishonour the recommendation of the DG ISI. A few days later, the Air Headquarters issued the signal of my posting as Second in Command (2 i/c) to No. 310 Wing, Chaklala. Commanded by Wing Commander Wajid Gilani, No 310 Wing was comprised of the Air Force Commandos. It was my best tenure of good relations with an Officer Commanding. I suppose there were two reasons for this: First, I found Wajid Gilani to be a person with great commanding qualities. Second, I was aware these were the last days of my Air Force service and wanted to leave on a happy note.

Before leaving the ISI, as customary, the Director General interviewed me again. At that time, General Kallu in his civil outfit occupied the office of the DG ISI. He made me sit in front of him and asked a few questions about the working conditions of my section.We had an interesting dialogue when, at the end, I asked him,

"Sir, am I permitted to ask you a question?"

He smiled and said with a kind gesture, "Sure."

I replied,

"Sir; I am sorry for trespassing, but I knew about every word written on the file of my release application." I paused, looked at him, and asked,

"Sir, why did you recommend my application when everyone below you had recommended against it? Moreover, you did not call me for an interview or ask me a word about my application."

Just then, the telephone in his office rang. I sat quietly as he talked on the phone with an occasional smiling glance at me. After disconnecting the phone, he smiled again and asked, "What was your question?"

I repeated my question and waited for the response. He said,

"With this much service, I can read the real issue between the lines." He thoughtfully added, "There is no point in keeping an officer if he has decided to leave the service. A Squadron Leader is mature enough to make that decision."

God bless his soul, General Kallu died after completing his tenure in the ISI.

*Z.A.Bhutto, Nawab Chatari, Abbas Huwaida (Foreign Minister of Iran) & Abboo Saheb in Isamabad*

*Shehansha Iran, Queen Farah Diba, Field Marshal*
*Ayub Khan, Mr. Wasti and Aboo Saheb*

*Abboo Saheb with Foreign delegates- Islamabad*

*Sitting from Left: Abboo Saheb, Mr. Wasti, Maj. Zameer Jafri, Mr. Shehzada and Mr. Rasheed and other staff of CDA Public Relations department.*

*From Left: Yawar, Dr. Sajjad, Group Captain Wajid and Nusrat*

*From Left: Dr. Cheema, Brigadier Hafeez, Khalid, Imran, Maj. General Bilal, Sir G.M. Shah, Nusrat, Brigadier Satti, Tahir Ikram, Raja Idrees, Mahmood and Mohsin sitting in front.*

*Nusrat and Captain Shahid*

*Nusrat and Ijaz Shafi Dining Night at Chaklala Air Base.*

*Field Marshal Ayub Khan and Abboo Saheb*

*Nusrat @ Bahrain Amiri Air Force*

*Before departure from Bahrain at Mamdooh's home- a
great host. From left Mrs. Wafa Mamdooh, Nusrat
and Shaheen- Mamdooh sitting in front.*

# Chapter Eleven

## The Bahrain Amiri Air Force (BAAF)

After retiring from the PAF, I spent time exploring the world and travelled to Europe and the USA. Settling in the USA on my terms proved unsuccessful. On returning to Pakistan after a few months, all attempts to establish a successful business failed as a result of implementing my own enterprising set of business values.

In August 1992, a team of the Bahrain Defence Force (BDF) visited Pakistan. They were looking for Air Traffic Controllers (ATCOs) to join their Air Force. Wing Commander Bilgrami and Squadron Leader Moazzam, both senior, had also retired at the same time. The three of us appeared together at the Karachi Fleet Club for a selection interview by a team from the Bahrain Amiri Air Force (BAAF). Wing Commander Bilgrami and Squadron Leader Moazzam went in first for the interview. When they came out, they informed me about the details of the offered contract - it was unacceptable. I felt it demeaning for officers of the PAF.

First Lieutenant Mamdooh-Al-Mohnnah of the Bahraini Selection team conducted the interview. When my turn came for the interview, I said,

"Sir, please do not offer me the contract that was offered earlier to the other two officers. I will not accept. However, I am thankful that you have come to my country. Let us forget about the contract. I invite you to be my guest at dinner if you are free tonight."

Mamdooh, a smart person, understood my message loud and clear. He did not even talk about the contract with me, but thanked me, refusing the dinner offer. He had another prior commitment for the night. However, he asked me to come back the next day with the other two officers. He promised to call his superior officers in Bahrain and work out a better contract. Pleased with the latest development, we left, hoping for the best. The next day, Mamdooh welcomed us and showed a much improved contract. We didn't get the exact desired contract, but we signed an agreeable one.

Wing Commander Fareed Bilgrami, Squadron Leader Moazzam Khan, and I became the first three officers of the PAF to join the ATC Squadron of the BAAF as Second Lieutenants. An officer of the rank of Lieutenant Colonel then acted as the Chief of Air Staff in Bahrain. Mamdooh-Al-Mohanna wore the rank of a First Lieutenant as the most senior officer of the ATC Squadron. He later proved to be a smart, intelligent, reasonable, and considerate commander.

In 1992, the BAAF had a small setup with a total strength of 650 personnel including all the airmen. Landing at Bahrain airport became our first experience in the country. A small island located off the eastern coastline of Saudi Arabia, it has a beautiful airport. With its capital in Manama, the island covers about 650 square kilometres with a population of over one million people. We enjoyed a comfortable flight on Gulf Air Lines operated by an efficient Bahraini crew. Our first interaction on land with the Bahraini customs and immigration staff left another positive impression about the people of Bahrain.

A Bahraini soldier in uniform who had waited outside the immigration counters drove us to Sheikh Isa Air Base in a military vehicle. Outside the airport in the open parking lot, the hot and humid weather welcomed us on that night in August 1992. On our trip from Bahrain International Airport to Shaikh Isa Air Base we travelled from one end to the other of the island of Bahrain. Disciplined traffic flowed on the surface of neat, clean roads that carried a few high-rise buildings on either side. About a two-hour flight away from Karachi existed a non-democratic country much less in area and population, but with a fantastic and disciplined environment. I at once shrugged off the thoughts that often bothered me in comparative analyses with Pakistan.

Our driver communicated in combined Urdu and English. We later discovered that the Bahrain population was mostly comprised of educated people. They spoke basic Urdu due to a large Indian community in the country. Indian nationals occupied every other department of service, but it was only the Pakistanis who wore the Bahraini Defence Forces uniform. The military driver dropped us off at the officers' mess of Shaikh Isa Air Base and handed us two room keys. For some odd reason he gave only one room key to Wing Commander Bilgrami and Squadron Leader Moazzam. They would be sharing a room. The key of a solo room came to my hand. Perhaps my balding hairstyle against the Bollywood hairstyle of Bilgrami and Moazzam impressed him. He considered me the senior officer who deserved to enjoy the solo room.

The air-conditioned rooms at the officers' mess carried decent furniture equivalent to any four-star hotel room; however, instead of an attached bathroom, there was only a sink. The community bathroom in the middle of the building reminded me of block 8 of the officers' mess at PAF Masroor. Officers of the American Army shared the building with us. We would meet them in the morning at the community bathrooms where they appeared in their birthday suits. Bathroom visits became an entertaining activity for us. We code-named those officers according to the size of their anatomical structures. The dining hall setting presented excellent attached recreation rooms with a television and some board games.

No. 1 Air Wing of Sheikh Isa Air Base housed two squadrons of the prestigious F-16 and F-5 aircraft. Except for a few American pilots, the Bahraini pilots flew the F-16 and F-5 aircraft. The ATC tower, a new modern structure equipped with the latest radio transmitters and the control panels for the runway lighting system, served the air traffic. We used the ATC jeep with the 'Follow Me' sign to inspect the runway and taxi tracks. A runway of more than 12,000 feet with a higher Load Classification Number (LCN) could accommodate the landing of any type of aircraft on its surface.

Below the Control Tower, the Approach Control Room was equipped with the latest radar system providing a vectoring service to the aircraft. Overall, this was a great ATC setup, much superior to the PAF Control Towers and rugged GCA radars.

Six BAAF officers worked as ATCOs when we reported to the base. First Lieutenant Mamdooh- Al-Mohanna soon promoted to Captain acted as the Senior Air Traffic Controller (SATCO) while First Lieutenants Sheikh Abdullah Al-Khalifa, Saad, Khalid Khalifa, Nasir Al Suadee, and Nizar formed the list of other controllers. Second Lieutenant Jasim and Adnan looked after the Riffa Air Base that was comprised of helicopters only.

Sheikh Abdullah-Al-Khalifa, a member of the royal family, impressed us with his conduct. He spoke with a soft voice and used decent words of communication giving proper respect to all. He often brought royal lunches to the tower. He enjoyed a close friendship with Second Lieutenant Nasir Al-Saudi. I remember him crying like a baby when Nasir died of illness. Sheikh Abdullah later became a helicopter pilot. We enjoyed wonderful coworker relations with all the Bahraini officers.

# Adrian and I

Adrian, an ex-Lieutenant Commander from the Royal British Navy, carried the title of ATC advisor. He had been a pilot of the Navy who later became an ATCO. At the Sheikh Isa Air Base, he controlled the approach radar operation. He attended all the high profile defence meetings with the higher command of the BDF. There existed an interesting rift between the uniformed and the non-uniformed personnel in the tower.

Adrian enjoyed three advantages over us Pakistani ATC officers and the other Bahraini Officers: first, his white English heritage; second, his on-the-type radar control experience; and third, his title of ATC advisor that somehow placed him above all other ranks of the ATC Squadron. However, a big disadvantage made him unhappy: our uniform. Despite being senior and an ex-military person, Adrian wore civilian clothes. He did not get the salutes and the title 'Sir' received by us officers in uniform. There were Bahraini soldiers in uniform who also worked in the ATC squadron. As per the normal military courtesy, they saluted and addressed us officers by 'Sir'. Adrian received more than double our salary, but was deprived of this prestigious facility. He was called by his first name and salutes were not extended to him. He felt it, too. Adrian had asked the Bahrain Defence Forces (BDF) Headquarters to give him the rank of a Major to run the ATC matters. They denied his request. Because of my adventurous nature, I often teased him by emphasizing my superiority of uniform. It strained our relations.

In the Pakistan Air Force, we had controlled flying of multiple squadrons getting airborne at the same time. Sheikh Isa Base had only two fighter squadrons. Controlling the flying of two squadrons was considered a piece of cake. However, Isa Air Base had the most modern radar equipment never before used by us. It required training to understand this modern radar equipment. Far from the rugged Ground Controlled Approach radar (GCA) of the Pakistan Air Force, this was some sleek equipment. Adrian was the only capable radar controller. He conducted our on-the-type training inside the radar room. My conflict with him amplified during training. Adrian declared me hard of hearing and sent me for a medical hearing test. I had to sit in front of a machine with a headset and a button to press every time I heard the tone. There wasn't a problem with my hearing and of course, I got a clean medical bill of health. But, I had become a bunny of Adrian. Inside the radar room, life became miserable. A stage arrived where my contract became vulnerable.

Captain Mamdooh-Al-Mohanna, Senior Air Traffic Control Officer (SATCO) and the boss, was a smart Bahraini officer. He realized the situation and appreciated the damage approaching the Bahrain Air Force. He wasn't prepared to bear the loss of a controller in whom the Bahrain Air Force had already invested so much time and money. He called me into his office downstairs and informed me of my posting to Riffa Air Base.

Riffa was a small helicopter base below the prestigious Sheikh Isa Air Base of F-16 and F-5 fighter jet aircraft. The difference between the two bases was like the difference between a fighter pilot and a helicopter pilot. Captain Mamdooh thought it would be a disgusting relegation not liked by me. However, deep inside, it made me feel happy. I could hardly hide my joy. I was reminded of the famous Urdu proverb, "Kubbay ko laat mari- uss ka kubb nikal gaya." It meant that a hunchbacked person, when kicked hard from behind, got rid of his hump. Anyone under similar circumstances would be grateful to the person who kicked away the hump. The same on-top-of-the-world feelings occupied my heart after hearing the news. But I acknowledged the news with apparent sadness on my face.

Adrian shook my hand helplessly when I smiled with a wink of an eye and bid him farewell at the Sheikh Isa Air Base. I was being posted away from the strong clutches of Adrian. I no longer had to attend the training in that dark radar room under his brutal control.

A five-minute drive from my home took me to Riffa Air Base compared to my thirty-minute morning drive to Sheikh Isa Air Base. Two other Bahraini officers, Second Lieutenant Jasim and Second Lieutenant Adnan who were both known for their carefree and friendly attitudes, served at Riffa Tower. With no difference in rank, pay, and all the other facilities, serving at Riffa Base remained a private dream for most of the ATC officers of Isa Air Base.

Riffa Air Base, home to the Helicopter Wing, housed the squadrons of AB-212, Bell AH-1E, and Black Hawk helicopters. First Lieutenant Saad, another Bahraini officer, got promoted to Captain and posted as SATCO Riffa Air Base. It upgraded the status of Riffa Tower.

Monthly Flight Safety meetings of the Air Force at the Riffa Air Base were attended by all the commanders of the Air Force. Adrian, in the capacity of ATC advisor, enjoyed the privilege of attending these meetings. Once, before going to the meeting, he came to visit the Riffa Control Tower. There wasn't any official reason for him to visit the Riffa Tower. He probably wanted to see the condition of his old bunny - me. I accorded him a good welcome and teased him in my peculiar style. In the heat of our argument Adrian said,

"Shut-up."

Though he said it in a frank manner, I made a big issue of this insult by a civilian to an officer of the Bahrain Air Force. I demanded an apology from him, but he left the tower to attend the meeting.

A general perception existed that Adrian used every opportunity to embarrass the officers in uniform. Following proper chain of command, I reported the matter to Captain Saad, the SATCO at the Riffa Tower. He at once called Captain Mamdooh at Sheikh Isa Air Base. Captain Mamdooh reported the matter to the higher command, who asked for a written report of the incident. I wrote an appropriate report and left it on the table - uncovered. After the meeting, Adrian came to the Control Tower again. Captain Saad also sat there. Adrian glanced at the report. He realized the seriousness of the matter and requested me not to forward the report. Adrian was well aware that he wouldn't be able to justify an official reason for his presence in the Riffa Tower. He could clearly see that his lucrative contract with the Bahrain Air

Force was in jeopardy. He implored me with many soft words, claiming that it was only a joke. In uniform, Captain Saad and I sat on the chairs with our legs stretched out on the table. Adrian kept standing and pleading. He requested me not to forward the report. Saad winked at me, signalling not to spare him. Adrian pressed so hard for a pardon it became difficult for me to say no to his request. Finally I said,

"Ok, Adrian, I am letting you go this time, but I hope you will be more careful next time." He thanked me many times before leaving the Riffa Tower that day.

Adrian never returned to the Riffa Control Tower during the next four years of my service with the BAAF. Captain Saad and I laughed and enjoyed our little chase with Adrian. I paid a goodbye visit to Adrian before leaving Bahrain in 1996. We shed our hard feelings over a pleasant cup of tea. He bid me farewell with good wishes and a broad friendly smile.

I found great company in the helicopter pilots at Riffa Air Base. I enjoyed my time controlling and visiting the helicopter squadrons. Lieutenant Colonel Atiya, a helicopter commander at Riffa, had trained at the Risalpur Academy of the PAF and remembered me from our cadetship days. Lieutenant Colonel Syed of the Black Hawk Squadron, Captain Nabeel, Captain Khalid, Captain Mubarik, and many other pilots became nice friends, and I enjoyed my time in their company.

A few times on my way to Pakistan I have made stop-overs at Bahrain. I enjoy meeting old friends and roaming around in a loveable country. I have no hesitation in saying that Bahrain is a beautiful country and the Bahrainis are magnificent people with open hearts.

# Pilgrimage - Makkah and Madina

My experience of the Pilgrimage (Hajj) performed during my stay at Bahrain will always be memorable. I share my experience here because of interesting incidents that occurred from the beginning to the end of Hajj. Islamic ritual of Hajj is an essential religious duty. Every Muslim man and women must perform Hajj once in their life time, provided they have sufficient wealth, health, and are also free of important family obligations. It includes about fifteen days of stay at Makkah and Madina associated with certain religious practices. Millions of Muslims gather every year in Makkah to perform this duty.

I had applied for immigration to Canada in 1995. Before the Hajj of 1996, the approval papers for my immigration arrived in Bahrain. I thought if I did not perform the Hajj from Bahrain, I would never perform it after settling thousands of miles away in Canada. When I gathered my financial resources, I realized that for expenses, I fell short of around 500 Bahraini Dinars (about 1500 Canadian dollars). I remembered that my wife had taken part in a committee with the families of the other Air Force officers working in Bahrain. A committee was a group of twelve people who contributed 50 Bahraini Dinars every month. Each of the twelve members had decided which particular month they would receive their share of the money. A total of 600 Dinars was collected and handed over to one member every month. They were free to use the money according to their requirement. This was a way to grow personal savings. The cycle lasted a year and by the end, everyone had received 600 Dinars at their allotted month. There wasn't any restriction on the use of committee money. Everyone was free to use that money according to his requirement. This month belonged to Flight Lieutenant Asif Dar to receive the 600 Dinar package. I called him to ask if he would exchange his turn for ours a month later. He at once agreed when I told him that the money would help me in performing the Hajj. This became a positive start.

Group Captain Farroq Nazmi, an ex-PAF officer and a very helpful person, lived next door. He worked at the BDF headquarters. He had already performed the Hajj, so I called him to find out about the procedure. Only a few days remained to the official start of the Hajj. Nazmi asked me if I intended to go the next year. When I told him I planned to go this same year, he told me that it was not possible at such short notice. He was right. The normal prevailing procedure spanned over a period of a few months to apply for leave, obtain a visa, and book accommodation at Makkah and Madina.

I called my boss Captain Mamdooh at Sheikh Isa Air Base. Because of the short time before the Hajj, Mamdooh asked me to report at once to his office at Sheikh Isa Air Base. I delivered the Hajj application the same day. Mamdooh recommended the leave application and asked me to take it to the office of the Chief of Air Staff, then a Lieutenant Colonel. I walked into the office of the Air Chief with my application. He congratulated me for taking the trip and wished me the best with the Hajj journey. He recommended my application to the BDF Headquarters and asked me to go to the office of the Brigadier General responsible for the final approval of the application and for the issuing of a letter of visa request to the Saudi Embassy in Bahrain. At the BDF Headquarters, they asked me to come after two days to pick up the letter to the Saudi embassy. A job that could take months under normal Bahraini military procedure was completed in a few hours.

I had applied for the Hajj visa for my entire family. My four children were young. Those of you who have performed the Hajj will know it was a lengthy exercise. Hotel rooms needed to be booked and transportation needed to be arranged a minimum of two months before the Hajj. Making no arrangements, I asked my wife to pack up the items required for a fifteen-day stay in Makkah and Madinah. My wife, used to such sudden departures, completed the task in a timely fashion.

We also informed our friends about our departure for the Hajj and our plans to look for a place to stay after reaching Saudi Arabia. My small Hyundai hatchback transported me in Bahrain. I had bought it from Fawad, a renowned perfumer and owner of the 'Syed Junaid Alam' chain of perfume stores in the Middle East. Fawad was the brother-in-law of Squadron Leader Shahzad

Ashraf from the PAF. He had helped by providing all the relevant information for settling down in Bahrain. When our families arrived from Pakistan, they also connected well with one another. Many PAF officers other than the ATC branch lived with their families and also served the BDF. We had formed a small community of families who often socialized and held parties regularly. Commander Naveed Malik from the Pakistan Navy, Colonel Ajmal from Pakistan Army, Doctor Mahmood, Doctor Khalid, Wing Commander Iftikhar, Wing Commander Riaz, Squadron Leader Ranjha, Squadron Leader Shahid, Ghias, Dar, Mr. Afzal Hundal, Mr. Riaz Malik and a few others formed this group. When I informed my friends and well-wishers about my Hajj plan they all gathered at my home in the evening. However, most of those present at my home that evening had NOT come to congratulate me or to bid me farewell for Hajj. Being worried for me, they had come to stop me from taking my children due to my insufficient arrangements made before the Hajj. All of them strongly recommended against taking the children on the Hajj trip. They offered to keep my children at their homes until our return to Bahrain.

My friend Fawad, the perfumer, also came that evening with his wife Ghazala, an excellent host and a well-educated lady from the University of Karachi. Fawad listened to the arguments of my friends and he too offered his place if I agreed to leave my children behind. I refused.

We would need twelve hours to drive to Makkah or Madina from Bahrain. I had been on this route before in my Hyundai hatchback and had performed an Umrah (a mini Hajj). Fawad warned me that the difference between the Umrah and the Hajj was like the difference between an ant and an elephant. When he realized that I wouldn't listen to anyone, he conveyed to me the message of his wife Ghazala, whom I respected like a sister. Fawad had a fleet of cars of the latest year parked at his home. That day he had come in a brand new Mazda MP van owned by his wife. He said that Ghazala would offer us her Mazda van for the journey to Makkah. Under the circumstances, that was an excellent offer, almost impossible to refuse, so I accepted it with gratitude. The seven-seat Mazda van provided us ample space to relax and elevated our morale. The next day I picked up my visa request letter from the BDF Headquarters and went to the Saudi Embassy in Manama. Only one person behind the window across the vacant hall waited for me. He at once stamped the visas on my passports and advised to exit Bahrain before sunset. The border was to be sealed following the standard Hajj procedure of entry into Saudi Arabia. I rushed back home, loaded our entire luggage into the back of our van, and crossed into Saudi Arabia before sunset on the same day.

I had decided to go first to Madina and then later to Makkah to perform the Hajj. With no prior arrangements, I headed for Madina in the Mazda MPV. My children enjoyed chatting their favourite prayers and songs in the back seats as we drove on the holy journey. We spent the night at a motel just short of Riyadh. The next day at dark we entered the holy city of Madina. Suddenly, I saw myself parked under the Pakistan House. I had stayed there before and had enjoyed my stay - it was like staying in the officers' mess accommodation of the PAF. I had called Pakistan House, Madina the day before my departure. They had informed me of the unavailability of rooms because of the visit of a Hajj delegation from Pakistan. I parked the van and went inside, hoping to find a place. To my great delight, the Hajj delegation had changed their plans and stayed at Makkah. We got the same grand bedroom we had stayed in before with six comfortable beds and a washroom. We stayed in Madina for a few days and left for Makkah two days before the start of the Hajj.

Makkah is a distance of about 500 kilometres from Madina and requires around five hours of driving time. About twenty miles short of Makkah, the Saudi authorities stopped us and asked to park our vehicle there. To control the influx of transport, only vehicles that carried twelve or more passengers could enter the city of Makkah. The Saudi government provided buses to Makkah. That came as a big shock for me. I had prepared myself to spend nights in the vehicle if we failed to find accommodation. My wife encouraged me and told me not to worry. We picked up our bags and boarded the bus, leaving the Mazda behind. The bus dropped us close to the holy mosque of Makkah that night. With four children, one wife, and four bags, I stood there in a vast ocean of human beings. People clad in the white Ahram dress were seen in all directions. The words of Fawad echoed in my mind: 'Umrah is an ant and the Hajj an elephant.' He was right.

I stood there helplessly when a passerby from Bangladesh asked me if I required a place to stay. After asking him for rates and the location, I asked him to show me the accommodation before I made a final decision. I left my wife and children there and followed him for about fifteen minutes through the crowded and unfamiliar streets of Makkah to a three-storey building. Lit with dim amber-coloured bulbs, every room carried about ten to fifteen people, with one washroom to serve them all. I wouldn't have stayed there with my family even if it was offered for free. We had come through the winding streets. I could never have found my family again if the one who had brought me didn't accompany me back. He was kind enough to bring me back to my family. We stood there waiting for a miracle.

After a short while, a Pathan from Pakistan arrived. He too was looking for people needing accommodation. I told him my clear requirement - a room with a minimum of six beds and an independent washroom. He asked me the duration of my stay. I told him I would be leaving Makkah the day after the Hajj. He gave me the best offer. His Arab boss had gone out of Makkah. A big air-conditioned storage area on the top third floor with an independent bathroom was available with the entire rooftop for our exclusive use. The storage area after inserting six beds turned into a penthouse. His only condition demanded us to vacate the penthouse within two days after the Hajj. The Arab boss was returning on the third day after the Hajj. I assured him we would vacate the penthouse on the day after the Hajj. He asked me not to waste time in first seeing the accommodation as he had given accurate information.

We hired a taxi parked close by and within half an hour found ourselves on the rooftop. Another half an hour wait converted the storage into a penthouse. We stayed there for the next ten to twelve days enjoying excellent boarding and lodging facilities.

The rest of the Hajj became a great spiritual journey which we enjoyed. When we returned to Bahrain after performing the Hajj, my friends did not believe me. Our fresh looks surprised them. I smiled at my friends who thought I had taken my family somewhere else on a picnic and made a false claim of performing the Hajj.

# Goodbye to Bahrain

My four years in Bahrain were loaded with wonderful life experiences. Involved in many activities, I played cricket and attended Mushairas (poetry recitations) and meetings of the Toastmasters club. We held sessions dedicated to understanding the message of the Quran by people of knowledge. Our many friends gathered to understand the wisdom of the holy Quran. My wife and children enjoyed attending and arranging parties in celebration of the many friendships we had formed all over Bahrain. We intermingled with the families of the Bahraini officers.

The salary offered by the Bahrain Air Force wasn't as great as that offered by other countries in the region, but the Bahraini people treated us with love and respect. I will always keep them on the top of my list. I left Bahrain for two reasons: One - my adventurous nature of exploring the world. Two - because I did not foresee a secure future and higher education for my children in Bahrain. Countries in the Middle East region offer no facility of citizenship in comparison to Western countries. The progress of the countries in the Middle East would have increased further if they had introduced a system of immigration for the people who worked there.

I applied for immigration to Canada after three years of stay in Bahrain. This application required me to submit a police clearance from my country of residence. If I applied for the police clearance, then I would have to disclose the reason for seeking it. It was not a crime, but I didn't think it appropriate to inform my employers. It would leave a bad impression on my employers if immigration was refused. I wrote to Canadian immigration and explained that as a defence officer in Bahrain, I was supposed to be security cleared; therefore, I could not submit the police clearance. Canada's immigration authorities agreed to my reason and exempted me from submitting the police clearance.

When my final immigration approval to Canada arrived, I picked up the telephone and first informed my boss, Captain Mamdooh. I told him I didn't want him to hear it from anyone else. I felt obligated to inform him first. He sounded sad at losing me, but understood my situation and wished us all the best. I served the proper notice in a timely fashion by not renewing my contract for the next term. Farewell parties continued for some time before we bid farewell to Bahrai with heavy hearts.

*Nusrat, Adrain, Nasir, Sheikh Abdullah and others*

*Mamdooh, Nusrat and Adrian
@ Sh. Isa Control Tower*

*Nusrat and Adnan @
Riffa Control Tower*

*From Left: Sh. Khalid, Nusrat and Mubarak*

*From Left: Mrs. Fawad, Mrs. Moazzam, Mrs. Nusrat,*
*Nusrat, Fawad, Moazzam and Ajmal*

*Families*

*BAHRAIN Families*

*Nusrat with Abboo Saheb*

*Mohsin with Abboo Saheb in New York*

*Qazi Fawad with Abboo Saheb and Ma Jee in Seattle*

*Abboo Saheb and Ma Ji with their children*

*From Left: Waqar, Shaheen, Nusrat, Maheen,
Mohib, Mahvish and Mohammed*

# *Acknowledgments*

I will remain indebted to my wife Shaheen and to my children Mohammed, Mohib, and Mahvish for putting up with me while I ignored them to work on the book. My daughter Maheen not only looked at the manuscript with her useful suggestions, but she also remained an active consultant and advisor throughout the completion of this project. Maheen also worked with my niece, Madhiya Qureshi in Karachi, in coming up with the initial design for the cover of the book. Madhiya beautifully illustrated my idea of the book cover. I am also thankful for the expert guidance and help of Mr. Arslan Sultan in Vancouver- he helped with the pictures and in shaping the cover design. I am thankful to my brother Kuckoo for his frank opinions and suggestions about the book's published excerpts.

Remarks on different excerpts of the book by the following seniors, juniors, coursemates, and friends kept me encouraged throughout the completion of this project:

Air Marshal Dilawar Hussain, Air Marshal Raashid Kalim, Air Marshal Zafar Mirza, Air Marshal Farhat Hussain, Air Marshal Asim Sulaiman, Major General Ahmed Bilal, Air vice-Marshal Abbas Mirza, Air vice-Marshal Shahid Nisar, Air vice-Marshal Atique Rafique, Air vice-Marshal Tubrez Asif, Air vice-Marshal Qasim Khan, Air vice-Marshal Sajid Habib, Air vice-Marshal Faiz Meer, Brigadier Asad Hakeem, Air Commodore Pervez Akhtar, Air

Commodore Amjad Bashir, Air Commodore Rana Sohail Asghar, Air Commodore Tanvir-ul-Islam, Air Commodore Raja Aslam, Air Commodore Nadeem Anjum, Air Commodore Kzaim Ali Awan, Colonel Amir Jalees, Colonel Atiq Malik, Col. Jawad Khan, Colonel Afzaal Niaaz, Group Captain Zulfiqar Khan, Group Captain Hyat Bangash, Group Captain Ejaz Minhas, Wing Commander Fareed Bilgrami, Wing Commander Sibghatullah Mudassir, Wing Commander Bahre Kamal, Wing Commander Shaharyar Shaukat, Wing Commander Amjad Rathore, Wing Commander Khalid Tamton, Wing Commander Najam Saeed, Wing Commander Shaukat Rasheed, Wing Commander Anwaar Hussain, and Wing Commander Hammed Qureshi.

Squadron Leader Shahid Ayaz, Squadron Leader Mahmud Ali Shah, Squadron Leader Adil Chaudhry, Squadron Leader Naeem ullah Khan, Squadron Leader Jamshed Ahmed, Squadron Leader Nawaz Khattak, Squadron Leader Mushtaq Chaudhry, Squadron Leader Yawar Kamal, Squadron Leader Shahid Hamid, Squadron Leader Javed Chaudhry, Squadron Leader Nabeel Mian, Squadron Leader Azizullah Qazi, Squadron Leader Khalid Khattak, Squadron Leader Ishtiaq Hussain, Squadron Leader Saqib Khawaja, Squadron Leader Naseem Rizvi, Squadron Leader Masood Ahmed, Squadron Leader Iqbal Shafique, Flight Lieutenant Nadeem Rasheed, and Pilot Officer Shahid Mahmud.

Mrs. Yasmeen Javed, Mr. Javed Rasheed, Mr. Sohail Siddiqui, Mrs. Nudrat Shamsi, Ms. Gail Tom, Ms. Sadia Raza, Mr. Irfan Malik, Mr. Abrar Ahmed, Mr. Khalid Iqbal, Mr. Obaid Rasul Qazi, Dr. Nayyer, Dr. Saeed Alam, Dr. Maqbool Cheema, Dr. Khalil Yaseen Shah, Qazi Fawad Ahmed, Mr. Nazeer Sadiq Janjua, Mr. Arshad Mir, Mr. Syed Shamim Haider, Mr. Nayyer Zaidi, Mr. Nadeem Zafar, Mr. Murtaza Zaidi, Mr. Raghbir Puri, Mr. Zarar Butt, Mr. Liaqat Bajwa, Mr. Mahmood Nawaz, Mr. Umair Gilani, Mr. Shaukat Khan, Mr. Syed Wajahat Shah, Mr. Sajid Baig, Mr. Imtinan Zameer, Mr. Khursheed Khan, Mr. Tauqeer Iqbal, Mr. Imran Khan Bangash, and Mr. Harpreet Singh.

Special thanks to Mr. Naseer Pirzada, Managing Editor of *The Miracle* newspaper; and to Mrs. Shahana Haqqi of *The Muslim journal* for publishing certain excerpts of *The Last Salute*.

I offer my gratitude to the expert team of Tellwell, comprised of Natasha Miller, Mitchel Anderson, Lenore Kennedy, and Jordan Mitchell.

I am also thankful to my copy editors Gary Ferguson from Auckland, New Zealand and Jen MacBride from Ontario, Canada.

Ultimately, I offer my extreme gratitude to all of my brother officers of the Pakistan Air Force and the Pakistan Army who richly shared their stories.

And finally, I am thankful to my readers who have gone through the pain and joy of reading this book. God bless you all.